Ben Crystal is an actor, author, and producer. He has worked in TV, film and thatre, and is a narrator for RNIB Talking Books, Channel 4 and the BBC. He co-wrote *Shakespeare's Words* (Penguin) and *The Shakespeare Miscellany* (Penguin) with his father David Crystal, and he is the author of *Shakespeare on Toast* (Icon). He lives in London and online at www.bencrystal.com

Adam Russ is an actor, writer, and presenter whose credits include *Eastenders*, *Holby City* and *Murphy's Law*. His previous books include *The Revenge Seekers' Handbook*, *101 Places Not to Visit* and *101 Sports Not to Try*.

Ed McLachlan's cartoons and illustrations have graced the pages of *Punch*, *Private Eye*, *The Spectator*, *The Oldie*, *Saga* and a host of magazines, books, greetings cards, calendars, and films.

SORRY, I'M BRITISH!

An Insider's Romp Through Britain from A to Z

Ben Crystal & Adam Russ

With cartoons by
Ed McLachlan

ONEWORLD

A Oneworld Book
Originally published by Oneworld Publications, 2010

This paperback edition published by Oneworld Publications, 2011
Reprinted 2014, 2015, 2016, 2019

ISBN 978-1-85168-856-2
eISBN 978-1-78074-040-9

Typeset by Glyph International, Bangalore, India
Cover Design by James Nunn
Printed and bound in Great Britain by Clays Ltd, Elcograf S.p.A.

Oneworld Publications
10 Bloomsbury Street
London WC1B 3SR
England

Stay up to date with the latest books,
special offers, and exclusive content from
Oneworld with our newsletter

Sign up on our website
www.oneworld-publications.com

Acknowledgements

From Ben Crystal

Thanks to my folks, for their constant support, feedback, and unerring ability to see what's not there. To Ed McLachlan, for being behind the book from day one and sketching to its heart. To Cathryn Summerhayes at William Morris Endeavour for just about everything. And to all at Oneworld for everything else.

And lastly, thanks to Will Sutton, for handing me a book in Amsterdam one December…

From Adam Russ

Thanks to Andrew Scott, a great writer and mine of amazingly useful trivia. His view that dropping "thou" from our language has given the British their naturally apologetic tone helped us find our title.

And to my wife, Lenna, for continually offering an impartial view on what makes Britain great. She could have chosen anywhere in the world to live, but thankfully for me, she chose here.

Introduction

The British are a funny bunch. When we're not queuing to pay our television licences or complaining about the weather forecast, we're very good at remedying every conceivable tragedy in human experience – by putting the kettle on for a nice cup of tea.

At least, that's the common understanding of us.

As it turns out, not that many of us would even call ourselves 'British'. Around ten million so-called Brits are more likely to declare themselves Scottish, Welsh, or (Northern) Irish, with many having fought hard for the right to be recognised independently.

Yet clearly there is much that unites the sixty-two million people of the ninth largest and third most populated island on Earth. Whether you're in the middle of one of the UK's sixty-five urban centres, or in splendid isolation on one of our 6000 islands and islets – and no matter which of the 400 languages you speak – there are still things that remain inherently British: the proliferation and variety of flags (few of which ever get flown); the rich pageantry and histories encoded in our coats of arms (that few understand the meaning of); and our bank holidays (that not all of the banks observe).

Our cuisine may range from an elaborate, eight-hour-to-cook Sunday Roast to the instant gratification of Fish and Chips or Beans on Toast, but our most popular meal is a dish that finds its origins on the other side of the world.

The British people generally consider themselves to be dignified, straightforward, and proud of their reluctance to express emotions – but the rule-book goes out of the window the minute a ball, a queue-jumper, or an against-all-odds chance of a medal are involved.

Having played such a large part in the spread of civilisation over the Western world, and had a hand in so many of the sports and entertainments that have become a staple part of other cultures, we now seem lost and separate from them all. In relinquishing the Empire on which the sun never set, we've become a mystery to others.

This book is a need-to-know guide, as much for the British as for visitors to Britain, the perfect companion when wandering lonely through the clouds of British behaviour.

Together, we'll explore the geographical oddities of the country, the bewildering beauty of its main language, and the emotions, sociology, and quiet eccentricities of its peoples.

From *sandwiches* to *superiority*, from *hoodies* to *hooliganism*, from *cricket* to *condiments*, and *Coronation Street* to *class*, this book will take you through the sometimes sarcastic, often poetic, generally polite, never boastful, but universally proud realm of all that's British – its culture, its institutions, and its people …

… and how you can get the most from your dealings with all three!

(With apologies for anything we've missed out.)

❧ ❈ A ❈ ❧

ALLOTMENTS

Many houses in Britain don't have gardens big enough, or land suitable enough to grow fruit, vegetables, and herbs. It's possible, however, to buy or (more normally) rent an allotment. Indeed, the National Society of Allotments and Leisure Gardeners Limited has been protecting, promoting, and preserving allotments since 1901.

Often found on the outskirts of towns or cities, a section of land will be run by the local council and be split up into equitably divided plots of land. Once gained, how you use your land and what you grow on it is up to you. Most people will invest in a shed to keep their tools, a kettle, cases of potato gin, and other necessities for sitting and watching the results of their hard work grow.

AMERICA

Britain's relationship with America might be described as 'special', but only if by 'special' we mean 'frequently dysfunctional'. Since the USA went its own way in 1776 the two nations have often found themselves in armed conflict, admittedly on the same side – but always on the USA's terms. Extradition treaties make it relatively easy for UK citizens to be deported to stand trial in the US, but the arrangement is strictly one-way.

While many of the residents of the White House and Ten Downing Street have shared obvious ideological alignments (Roosevelt and Churchill in the 1940s) and even genuine mutual affection (Reagan and Thatcher in the 1980s) these bonds have been the obvious exceptions rather than the general rule.

Culturally, however, the bonds run deep. All Brits share a perverse delight in correcting Stateside mangling of the English language and a despair at the (relative) blandness of American music. American

television generally fares better, though we've probably all had enough of *Friends* now.

ANGEL OF THE NORTH

Located in the Tyneside town of Gateshead, Anthony Gormley's 20-metre high, 54-metre wide, steel sculpture has had a huge impact since its unveiling in 1998. As far as public art goes, this is about as public as it gets – the Angel can be seen from the nearby motorway, as well as from East Coast trains bound for York and London to the south, and Newcastle and Edinburgh to the north.

Despite the to-be-expected controversy and questions surrounding its design and meaning, it has rapidly become an important landmark

and totem for the region. Both its permanence and placement make it hugely accessible for anyone journeying by.

The fact that the Angel was built in Hartlepool has also given the residents of that seaside town reason for particular pride. Before the Angel, Hartlepool was best known for charging a shipwrecked monkey with the offence of spying for the French during the Napoleonic wars. The monkey was found guilty and hanged.

ANNUS HORRIBILIS

The year 1992 saw the effective end of not one, but two royal marriages. Diana, Princess of Wales marked her departure from the centre stage of monarchy with a tell-all book, and Sarah Ferguson promptly followed suit with a paparazzi-photographed poolside romp with a Texan banker.

So, somewhat bemused, Her Majesty the Queen was already having a tough old time of it when one of her favourite homes, Windsor Castle, caught fire.

Four days later, during her recorded Christmas message at London's Guildhall, she referred to her less than enjoyable year as her *annus horribilis*, and another Latin phrase was able to sneak its way into popular parlance.

ANTHEMS

Wherever they are heard, the Welsh, Scottish, and Northern Irish anthems – 'Land of My Fathers', 'Flower of Scotland', and 'Londonderry Air' respectively – are sung with passion and commitment.

Meanwhile, the British anthem 'God Save the Queen' will most commonly be sung sotto voce, in an apologetic, hesitant tone. This may be down to the fact that the English – whose anthem it effectively is – are less renowned for their singing than their Welsh, Scottish, or Northern Irish neighbours.

Perhaps many of them prefer to save their voices for more tuneful but equally patriotic ditties such as Elgar's 'Land of Hope and Glory' or Blake's 'Jerusalem', both of which already serve as unofficial anthems for the UK. Or perhaps those present – be they from Belfast, Glasgow, Cardiff, or London – are simply petrified that they will be expected to keep singing beyond the first verse. Less than a fraction of one per cent of the British population know the full lyrics of the second and third verses:

O Lord, our God, arise,
Scatter her enemies,
And make them fall.
Confound their politics,
Frustrate their knavish tricks,
On Thee our hopes we fix,
God save us all.

Thy choicest gifts in store,
On her be pleased to pour;
Long may she reign:
May she defend our laws,
And ever give us cause
To sing with heart and voice
God save the Queen.

Apologies

If the British could make anything other than queuing an international sport, then apologising would be it. Sadly, this does not mean the British are especially polite.

Most of Asia would top Britain's medal haul in the Impeccable Manners Olympics, and just about everywhere else on the planet offers better customer service. But in terms of sheer *volume* of apologies, the British lead the field, with the English in particular devoted to the practice of over-apologising, usually for things beyond their control.

Across every part of Britain, 'sorry' seems to be the best way to start a sentence, usually when no apology is intended, viz. 'SORRY, but would you mind moving that ...?'

'Appropriate'

The essentially meaningless adjective at the heart of the philosophy of Political Correctness.

In everyday usage, to be deemed 'inappropriate' (in dress, behaviour, or even opinion) is to have committed a cardinal sin. Ignorance of the unspoken rules decreeing what is 'appropriate' for a given situation is no defence, and disputing the grounds on which you've been subjectively judged is only likely to make matters worse, and to be considered 'inappropriate'.

Increasingly though, many organisations are becoming more prescriptive as to what constitutes 'inappropriate'. In 2009, a branch of Tesco in Cardiff effectively became the first supermarket in Britain to introduce a dress code for its customers. It put up notices stating that footwear was compulsory and prohibited shoppers from turning up in their nightwear.

ARCHITECTURE

The influence of the Romans lingers in the ruins of Hadrian's Wall, the straightness of London's Oxford Street, and the abundance of many (beautiful but now pointless) aqueducts.

However, most architectural histories of Great Britain see the Norman influence as the first important stage – possibly because of the number of stunning examples still to be seen today.

Below is a handy guide to the major styles in British architecture over the last thousand years...although when it comes to the last century, your own guess as to what's going on is probably as good as anyone else's.

Architectural Style	Approximate Dates	Defining Characteristics	Notable Examples
Norman	1066–1485	Function over form, imposing	Durham Cathedral, Tower of London, Chepstow Castle
Tudor	1485–1603	Open and ostentatious	Hampton Court Palace, Pembroke Court Palace, Edinburgh Castle
Baroque	1604–1714	Ornamental, European influenced	St Paul's Cathedral, Blenheim Palace, Duff House in Banff
Georgian	1714–1840	Simplicity and symmetry	Armagh Mall, The Royal Crescent in Bath, Balbirnie House in Fife

Victorian	1840–1901	Mythic and ornamental	Houses of Parliament in Westminster, Glasgow City Chambers, Aston Webb Building in Birmingham
Modernist/ Post-Modernist/ Post-Post-Modernist	1901–	Function over form. Again. Or not. Anything goes, really.	The Gherkin in London, Holyrood Parliament Building in Edinburgh, Waterfront Hall in Belfast, Wales Millennium Centre in Cardiff

ARGENTINA

Two key factors have got in the way of Britain and Argentina exchanging Best Friends Forever bracelets:

- the sovereignty of the collection of 700 tiny South Atlantic islands known as the Falklands or Las Malvinas respectively;
- Maradona's handball in the 1986 World Cup match against England.

Despite the enmity that clearly exists on a diplomatic level, Argentineans can expect a warm welcome from a vast majority of Brits should they visit the UK. This is mainly because Maradona's blatant cheating was no doubt cheered throughout parts of Scotland, Wales, and Northern Ireland. But it did give English fans something to moan about, and they're never happier than when they're whining about being cheated out of a victory.

ARGOS

Founded in 1973 and a notable survivor of every ensuing retail recession, Argos has built its success around a single book – its catalogue. Estimated to be found in two-thirds of British homes, the same catalogue (albeit in a heavily ring-bound and securely laminated form) is on display in every branch, in place of any actual products.

An odd hybrid of mail-order, internet, and department-store shopping, purchases are made electronically by order number (gained from the biblical catalogue); promptly dispatched by a hidden warren of warehouse staff; then finally collected by eagerly waiting customers.

Despite its permanence on the British high street, its work supporting a number of charities, and a steadfast refusal to be tempted to alter the core of its business model, Argos has never quite shaken off its downmarket associations.

As a result, a trip to a branch tends to be tolerated rather than enjoyed. Still, if you really, *really* need to buy a lawnmower, a set of carving knives, a two-man tent, and a footbath – and you only have fifteen minutes – you can do it in Argos.

ARGUING

British people tend not to argue. They disagree a *lot*. But the volume at which objections are raised means they rarely qualify as full-on rows.

British disagreeing also involves the use of as many placatory statements as possible, partly to avoid causing offence, and partly because both parties are usually as concerned with taking the moral high ground as they are with getting their point across.

'Yes, I hear what you're saying, and while that used to be the case, I think you'll find that's no longer true …'

'Well, with all due respect, I think you'll find that it is, in fact I'm certain.'

'OK, well you might be right, but I'm pretty sure that it's changed quite recently. I know I was surprised when I found out.'

'Look, we've been friends a long time, and you know I'd never knowingly contradict you. I do totally understand where you're coming from – but I really think you might be wrong on this …'

And so on.

As with many aspects of British behaviour, the rules all change once alcohol is involved.

'ARSE'

The British word for the part of the body you sit down on is one of many mild profanities that serve a variety of useful functions. None is likely to get you into too much trouble – as long as it's not used in formal surroundings.

As a noun, it stands in for *idiot*; as a verb – 'arsing about' – it suggests pointless or inept behaviour; and in its adjectival form – 'An arsing bunch of idiots!' – it's a brief and damning critique.

Finally, on its own as an expletive, it provides any Brit with a more acceptable outcry than 'shit', and is most famously delivered in British culture by Father Jack from the hugely popular television programme *Father Ted*.

ASBO

Introduced in 1998, the Anti-Social Behaviour Order was designed to curb everyday illegality without having to clog up the judicial system. Noise pollution, drunken conduct, and fly tipping were three of the offences ASBOs were intended to tackle, but they have since been issued for everything from games of street football to unlicensed wheel clamping.

Penalties for recipients range from curfews and prohibitions on entering certain areas, to what clothes the ASBO-receiver may wear, or even what vocabulary he or she may use.

The ongoing rise has led to some recipients embracing 'ASBO Culture', where the issuing of an order is seen an inevitable consequence of their situation, or even a badge of honour.

A pitbull shot dead by police marksmen in Mitcham (south London) in 2008 after it attacked four people, had been named ASBO by its owner.

ASCOT (ROYAL)

For one week of every year, Her Majesty the Queen is spared the ordeal of state school visits and ceremonial openings of ball-bearing factories.

Royal Ascot may not be the zenith of the flat-racing season for the sport's true aficionados, but it is certainly the social centrepiece, with crowds of around 300,000 descending on the Berkshire racecourse.

A small proportion of these join the Royal Family in the Royal Enclosure, a VIP area designed to keep away disgruntled punters such as Dennis Collins – who was transported to Australia for throwing a rock at King William IV at the 1832 meeting.

The strict dress code expected within the enclosure has helped ensure the entire event is as famous for the fashion on display as for the equine activity, particularly on Ladies Day. But for at least one person, all of this is secondary – Her Majesty's own horses have an outstanding record of winning at Ascot.

ASTON MARTIN

The most famous British motoring marque. The car's fame has benefited mainly from links to James Bond (before he was played by an Englishman), Prince Charles (before he got all Green), and a fiercely proud tradition of automotive manufacture in the UK (when it still happened).

Aston Martin's fortunes have in many ways mirrored those of the UK home-grown industry as a whole over the last fifty years – a general decline. However, its purchase by a UK-headed consortium in 2007, a new test centre at the world famous Nürburgring circuit, and a triumphant turn at the Le Mans Series Championship in 2009, all suggest the promise of a bright future.

AUTOMATICS

Cars in the UK are predominantly manual, rather than automatic. For anyone unused to a gearstick and clutch, the greatest challenge is likely to be starting the car on an incline – achieved by balancing the pressure held on the clutch and the accelerator pedals. To be able to do so successfully is often seen by the British as something to be proud, even boastful of.

As a result, automatic cars are held to be little better than fairground dodgem cars. Automatics are still readily available to buy – if you're unable to summon the vast talent and expertise needed to master a manual gearbox.

AXMINSTER

A town in south-west England, the name is particularly famous for a brand of high-quality carpet that has been made there since the eighteenth century.

Now made all over the world, the name Axminster has become a more generic term for a carpet of superior quality. Custom designs and styles can still be ordered from the original company in Devon.

❧❀ B ❀❧

BANK HOLIDAYS

The 1871 Bank Holidays Act awarded the British a series of paid days off work, many of which seem to have been chosen entirely at random.

Many, however, were chosen by very important people to coincide with big meetings in the village cricketing calendar.

While the English and the Welsh have accepted these ever since, the Northern Irish and Scots have understandably picked days that actually mean something to them to celebrate. And also managed somehow to wangle some extra time off into the bargain.

So, the Scots get less excited about Easter, but give themselves an extra day to recover after New Year. Both the Irish and the Scots take a day to celebrate their national saints, while the Welsh wave flowers and the English grumble about the April showers.

Moves to put the English and Welsh on the same par by giving them their Saint's Day off have been promised. For the English, this would mean a day off to celebrate the legendary victory in combat of a

Christian knight with a murky past over a fire-breathing creature that almost certainly never existed.

New Years Day	**1 January**
2 January (Sc)	
Saint David's Day	**1 March***
(Patron Saint of Wales)	
Saint Patrick's Day	**17 March**
(Patron Saint of Ireland) (NI)	
Saint George's Day	**23 April***
(Patron Saint of England)	
Good Friday	**Friday before Easter Monday, between 22 March and 25 April**
Easter Monday	**between 22 March and 25 April**
Easter Tuesday (NI)	**between 22 March and 25 April**
Early May Bank Holiday	**first Monday in May**
Victoria Day (Sc)	**3rd Monday in May**
Spring Bank Holiday	**last Monday in May**
Orangeman's Day (NI)	**on or after 12 July**
Summer Bank Holiday (Sc)	**first Monday in August**
Summer Bank Holiday	**last Monday in August**
(Eng, NI, Wa)	
Remembrance Day	**11 November***
Saint Andrew's Day	**30 November**
(Patron Saint of Scotland) (Sc)	
Christmas Day	**25 December**
Boxing Day	**26 December**

* denotes a day of celebration, but not a bank or public holiday.

Although these days are known as Bank Holidays, many establishments and businesses stay open, and the greatest banking issue is likely to be cashpoints running out of notes.

Timing of the Easter weekend changes every year, but generally will fall on the first Sunday which follows the first full moon after 21 March. But not always.

BAKED BEANS (HEINZ)

Sold in Britain by the American company Heinz since the late nineteenth century, this is an essential and savoury part of the British diet. A traditional full English Breakfast will certainly include Baked Beans, and a lunch of them liberally served over buttered toast is still popular.

Although Heinz faces increasing competition – notably from Branston, another favourite British brand – it produces a staggering 1.5 million cans of beans every day.

'BAR (CALLED TO THE)'

The most notable feature of British legality for most remains its attachment to the ancient past. Witness the archaic language in use; the age of the presiding judges; and the attire of those legal eagles 'called to the bar' – that is, qualified to participate in legal proceedings – at the highest courts in the land.

While it may seem odd to foreigners that these lawyers practise in flowing robes and funny little wigs, the somewhat arcane nature of their dress reflects a notable few survivals on the UK statute books. For example, laws which make it illegal to eat a mince pie on Christmas Day, to put a stamp on a letter upside down, or to die in the Houses of Parliament.

BBC

Founded in 1922, with a remit to 'inform, educate, and entertain', the British Broadcasting Corporation is unique among the world's media empires. Or so it keeps telling anyone who'll listen. Or watch.

Receiving the lion's share of a licence fee charged to every household with a TV set, the BBC has never been short of money to spend on quality programmes, though changes to its funding seem imminent.

Rising competition, a falling audience share, and the means to watch programming without a TV have all tested the entire concept of the licence fee. Despite these tensions, elements of the Corporation's work continue to set benchmarks that are aspired to the world over.

Meanwhile, the focus on improving audience share and incessant adverts for its own output has left many wondering just what the difference between the BBC and the rival commercial stations is anyway.

BEATLES (THE)

Collectively now worth more than £1 billion, the tragically early deaths of John Lennon and George Harrison have meant that only the left-handed members of the group are alive to enjoy it. Still, the Beatles are more successful than ever, as Paul McCartney and Ringo Starr find themselves the closest thing to respected royalty in the UK.

Lovingly remastered reissues of their work have meant regular appearances in the chart for the band that split in 1970, and tacky unlicensed memorabilia are available not just in Liverpool, but anywhere the Fab Four have had even the vaguest association with.

The original Cavern Club may have become a car park and Ringo's childhood home may have been slated for demolition, but legions of fans still besiege the zebra crossing featured on the group's Abbey Road sleeve.

Driving by the Abbey Road Studios is never a good idea – the queue of cars is usually outnumbered by the hordes of dawdling tourists momentarily standing stock-still on the crossing.

BEER

When Brits say 'beer', they are using a generic term for both lager and ale, despite the fact that the two are quite different.

Lager is light in colour, effervescent, ferments at 4–13°C, is served at 4–8°C and was first brewed in Bavaria in the sixteenth century. Ale, or 'bitter', is fermented at warmer temperatures (18–22° C), served at 12–14°C, and tends to be darker and less effervescent. It's more closely related to the kind of thing a Viking visitor to British shores would have knocked back after a hard day's pillaging.

Lager in the UK tends to have international branding – frequently Germanic – while bitter has an alarmingly diverse assortment of names to reflect its idiosyncratic style, such as Bishop's Finger, Old Leg Over, and Ye Olde Trout.

The consumption of bitter was overtaken by lager for the first time in 1997, but the devotion of the British to the darker alcohol remains deeply felt, judging by the continued growth in membership of the Campaign for Real Ale (CAMRA).

BELFAST

Once at the core of the Troubles (1969–2001), Northern Ireland's capital is a relatively peaceful place now, but this is a recent development. Anyone wanting to see the remarkable political murals painted on the sides of houses in East Belfast should do so with the greatest respect. Memories of bombings on the city's main streets and constant Army patrols are still fresh.

The actions of both loyalist and republican paramilitary forces – and of the security services themselves – claimed more than 3500 lives in Northern Ireland. While political issues remain to be resolved, and acts of violence do still occasionally occur, the end of the bloodshed is a long overdue achievement for the people of Belfast.

BIRMINGHAM

Along with Manchester and Liverpool, the city of Birmingham was one of the frontrunners of the Industrial Revolution – reflected by its place in the UK's transport network.

Not only bordered by the M6, M42, and M5 motorways (and the notorious spaghetti junction where the M6 meets the A38), Birmingham also boasts more miles of canal than the city of Venice.

Home to the longest urban bus route in Europe and the Crufts International Dog Show, and birthplace of Black Sabbath and Duran Duran, Birmingham was for many years derided for its gloomy central precinct – The Bull Ring. This was completely refurbished in 2008/09 and the city is reinventing itself as a central commercial venue, with an increasingly vibrant cultural life.

BLACK WEDNESDAY

Losing the taxpayers' money in spectacular fashion is something British governments have always excelled at, but 16 September 1992 remains a notable low in the UK's economic history.

Short selling of sterling – selling with a view to rebuying later at a lower price – forced Britain to withdraw from the European Exchange Rate Mechanism less than two years after joining it. It also cost the UK taxpayer an estimated £3.4 billion.

Politically, the events put a big dent in the Conservative government's reputation for financial competence. That said, the subsequent Labour government proved themselves to be equally adept at wasting cash, most notably in their 1999 decision to sell half the UK's gold reserves, when gold prices were at their lowest for a decade. The cost of that decision to UK taxpayers? Around £2 billion.

'BLESS YOU'

The appropriate response when someone sneezes. Short for 'God bless you', the phrase can be used despite anyone's particular religious beliefs.

Ironically, considering the theological implications, there is a curious superstitious attachment – if the sneezer says 'thank you' after being 'blessed' by the sneezee, it is considered by many to be bad luck.

BLITZ/DUNKIRK SPIRIT

It says something about the British that the episodes of World War II most frequently alluded to are not heroic victories, but an onslaught that was endured, and a makeshift retreat.

In both cases the quiet heroism of people pulling together and making the most of limited resources – while carrying on as if everything was actually normal – is seen as key to what's best about the British character.

The hardships suffered by the generations who lived through the war, and then on through rationing (which didn't end until Midnight on 4 June 1954), now seem to be a rapidly fading memory.

Claims to having a Blitz or Dunkirk spirit are still frequently made by the pampered generations that followed. Usually, though, when stoically accepting that their iPod battery has run out of charge.

BONFIRE NIGHT

While the burning of scrapwood and detritus gained from a day's gardening is an everyday occurrence, Bonfire Night is a uniquely British anniversary, celebrated on or around 5 November.

Just whether it's the attempt to blow up the Houses of Parliament in 1605 (the Gunpowder Plot) that Brits are celebrating – or the failure of Guy Fawkes and his co-conspirators to see their plan through – no one seems to know. But it's a good excuse for a party, fireworks, and the last barbeque of the year.

The burning of an effigy of Guy Fawkes is far less central to the evening than it once was, though enterprising children will still display their creations in the weeks preceding the 5th (often in wheelbarrows) and requesting a 'Penny for the Guy'. Much like the magpie rhyme (see 'Magpies'), something you'll hardly ever hear, but everyone knows off-by-heart is the associated nursery rhyme:

> Remember, remember the fifth of November
> Gunpowder, treason and plot,
> I see no reason why gunpowder treason
> Should ever be forgot.

BOWLER HATS

A round, hard felt hat, that came into fashion in the mid-nineteenth century, and replaced the top hat, which was taller and less firm. British men used to wear bowler hats. They don't any more.

BOXING DAY

Also known as St Stephen's Day, 26 December was named after the boxes of gifts and donations left in churches, to be given out to the poor.

Good King Wenceslas famously performed an act of charity on this day, and Boxing Day is when many British families will open their house to friends and neighbours, generally having kept to themselves the day before. None of which has much to do with St Stephen, who was stoned to death for blasphemy in AD 35.

BRISTOL

The seat of the early 1990s trip-hop movement, where the likes of Massive Attack and Portishead took Britain's music in a very different direction from Manchester's guitar-driven bands.

At the end of the estuary between south-west England and south Wales, Bristol's historic docks were a focal point in Britain's import and slave trades in the seventeenth century. More recently, its most notable commercial activities have been within the high-tech and aeronautical industries – Concorde made its first ever flight from Bristol Filton Airport.

In 2008 the city was named Britain's 'most sustainable city' by environmental charity Forum for the Future, based on recycling, future-proofing, and the quality of life enjoyed by its citizens.

BRITISH ISLES

The geographical name for the lands and islets that include and surround England, Ireland, Scotland, and Wales. The mainland is the ninth largest island in the world, and the third most populated.

It is surrounded by 6228 islands and islets, and goes by many names, from the political (The United Kingdom of Great Britain and Northern Ireland) to the colloquial (Great Britain/UK) and the historical (Britannia) (see United Kingdom).

BRITPOP

A musical subgenre notable for its chirpy guitar tunes. The term Britpop also refers to a brief period of history when an imminent and long overdue change in government coincided with the commercial rise of a number of UK bands, notably Blur and Oasis.

The surrounding atmosphere of expectant excitement helped fuel a seemingly fierce but largely media-created musical rivalry between 'northern' Oasis and 'southern' Blur. From then on, any British act with a guitar player in its line-up was labelled as 'Britpop'. Fortunately for the rest of the world, this cultural smugness was mercifully short-lived.

By the time Tony Blair was elected in 1997, the Britpop tag was already losing its lustre. Blur moved into increasingly experimental musical territory, which would ultimately lead to schisms within the group, and their inevitable split came during the recording of their final studio album in 2002, although they reformed for a string of live shows in 2009. Oasis stayed in exactly the same place musically, accepted an invitation to Downing Street to meet the new PM, and kept recording long after they should have stopped.

BROWN SAUCE (HP)

Britons fall into two select, rival camps: those who prefer tomato ketchup with their food, and those who prefer brown sauce. Using malt vinegar as a base, HP has a fruity taste. Originally made by HP Foods, it is now owned by its old nemesis, Heinz, who retained the distinctive branding and prominent image of the Houses of Parliament on the label.

This has proved to be a source of irritation for many Britons, as HP is no longer made in the UK. Production of HP was transferred to the Netherlands in 2007, and the factory in Aston where it had been made has been closed and demolished.

BRUSSELS

The effective capital of the European Union, Brussels is usually blamed for being the source of the UK's most unpopular, unworkable, and unlikely laws.

Regardless of whether they are European directives or not, unfavourable regulations on vegetable shapes, working hours, or pet ownership will be referred to as having originated in the Belgian capital, often prefixed by the alliterative 'barmy'.

BSE (MAD COW DISEASE)

Bovine spongiform encephalopathy, the fatal disease affecting adult cattle, was first recognised in British cattle in the mid-1980s. Its origin is unknown, but the leading theory is that it came from feeding the cows a protein made from diseased sheep offal.

British farmers endured a horrific few years as a result of the outbreaks, and many farms are still recovering. Happily, the improvements in regulatory standards within the agricultural industry – and thereby the quality of the beef – are now higher in the UK than ever before.

Builder's (tea)

Asking a Brit if he or she wants a cup of tea used to be a simple enough affair. But the rise of herbal tea and huge growth in popularity of blends such as Earl Grey has made it slightly more complicated.

For anyone who doesn't want a herbal/obscure/exotic blend, there's only one answer: 'Builder's'.

To truly qualify as 'Builder's' the teabag must be left in the hot water for a relatively long time to ensure both a very strong flavour and a dark-tan colouring. The 'Make Mine a Builders' brand teabag was launched in 2007 with claims it was faster brewing than conventional teabags. Tetley don't seem worried.

Canals

Britain's 2500 miles of canals were once the commercial highways of the country, but competition first from the railways and then the roads led many to fall into disuse and decay. The success of organisations such as the Inland Waterways Association in supporting the restoration and maintenance of around two-thirds of the network is largely down to the post-war growth of boating within the leisure industry.

The attraction of gently pottering along on the water, making frequent stops at waterside pubs, is not peculiar to the British. Hollywood action star Harrison Ford enjoyed four days piloting a narrow-boat on the Llangollen canal in 2008, where he is reported to have pushed his 60ft rental up to speeds of almost 4mph.

Car boot sales

Where the notion that stuffing the back of your car with junk you no longer want, driving to a car park filled with dozens of other like-minded individuals, and selling said junk to each other originally comes from, is unknown. But it's a popular British weekend occurrence anyway.

CARDIFF

Nestled in the south of the country, the Welsh capital city is home to the neo-gothic splendour of Cardiff Castle and the equally magnificent Millennium Stadium.

Buffalo Bill was a regular visitor with his wild west show in the 1890s, and Laurel and Hardy performed at the city's Philharmonic Concert Hall in the 1940s – but the well-earned Welsh reputation for hospitality means that celebrity status is not required to receive a warm welcome. Said welcome will often be accompanied by some of the finest baritone singing you're ever likely to hear.

CCTV

First used in 1942 to monitor a V11 rocket launch site in Germany, Closed Circuit Television cameras are now more common than public payphones on the streets of Great Britain. There is now one camera for every fourteen members of the UK population.

CCTV's principal use has been to capture instances of minor, traffic-related infringements. While the documentary evidence they provide may also help in the fight against crime, for many they represent the growth of an overbearing surveillance society in the UK.

In 2007, a cub-scout leader was taken to court by Merseyrail after CCTV evidence from an enforcement officer's headcam showed her resting her feet on the seat opposite. Chester Magistrates gave her – and seven other offenders – an absolute discharge.

CEILIDH

A lively social gathering (pronounced KAY-lee), not only found in Scotland and Northern Ireland, but right across the UK.

The central elements of ceilidhs have remained the same for generations: upbeat Gaelic folk music played on traditional instruments – accordion, drum, fiddle, flute, and bodhran, among them. The second element: dances with suitably evocative names – The Polygamous Reel, The Drongo, The Dashing White Sergeant, and The Gay Gordons.

Credit is awarded for enthusiasm rather than ability when it comes to the dancing.

CHARACTERS

Here are ten characters whose appeal worldwide has helped shape the world's view of Britain and the British:

James Bond – English MI6 spy, most famously played by a Scot.

Harry Potter – box office blockbusting boy wizard, beloved more by adult muggles than by their children.

Sherlock Holmes – most filmed movie character. And opium-smoker.

Macbeth – Scottish king often played, but never mentioned, in theatres.

Winnie the Pooh – honey-loving bear who wasn't always American …

Ebenezer Scrooge – miserly accountant haunted by his past – who wasn't always a duck. Or surrounded by Muppets.

Jeeves – erudite valet, saddled with a brainless dandy.

Miss Marple – sprightly pensioner sleuth of fourteen Agatha Christie novels.

Robin Hood – forest-dwelling outlaw, whose philanthropy was probably too good to be true.

Mr Bean – epitome of British social ineptitude, loved the world over.

'CHAV'

Geordies were referring to 'charvas' for a decade before the UK media got hold of the word. They soon turned it into a convenient label to be

applied to any individual/product/act/social group that they wanted to sneeringly look down on.

As with all such subjective labels, the defining characteristics will vary wildly from case to case. But by its continued existence – and popular usage – it serves as a reminder that while the British class system has changed a great deal in the last century, it's still alive and well. The wearing of designer labels – however expensive – is no way to graduate from its ranks.

CITY OF LONDON/THE SQUARE MILE

London's financial district occupies just over one square mile, radiating out from the Bank of England. While the boundaries of the 'City' were once imaginary, a series of high-profile terrorist attacks in the 1990s led to the establishment of a 'ring of steel' of security around it, comprising surveillance cameras, traffic chicanes, manned concrete enforcements – but remarkably little actual steel. While the City boasts a number of attractions, fine restaurants, and notable architecture, it's best avoided between 7am and 9.30am and from 4pm to 7pm. That is, unless you're in the mood for competing for pavement and tarmac space with its workforce, who are aggressive and fast moving even by London standards. Admiring the architecture, dawdling, or otherwise getting between City staff and their way home is highly inadvisable.

By contrast, the City is almost entirely empty at weekends, though should you choose to visit it on a Sunday you'll probably want to take supplies with you: ninety per cent of the pubs, bars, restaurants, and shops will be shut, along with the financial houses they serve, once the regular working week is done.

CLASS

Successive governments have claimed that Britain is now a 'classless society'. This is either a convenient lie, or hopelessly naive – class remains the dominant force in shaping the way the British view themselves and others. Any and all attempts to replace the old class distinctions have met with mixed success.

The National Readership Survey system uses a combination of earning power, profession, and education to split the middle class three ways, from B (professional, middle managerial) to C1 (clerical and junior managerial) and C2 (skilled manual).

This may be a useful tool for marketeers or sociologists, but most Brits still refer to the old Upper/Middle/Working model, with one significant addition. If you are unable to avoid getting into a discussion about class, the following should help you in determining where you and the rest of your social circle lie:

Upper Class. Anyone with links to royalty or old money, probably with a country estate and a decrepit Land Rover. Must have been publicly schooled, can work but doesn't have to, and frequently doesn't need to. Accent can be anything from extreme RP ('received pronunciation' – the speech of the establishment and monarch) to outright mockney (fake cockney, e.g. Guy Ritchie).

Middle Class. Anyone whose work doesn't involve getting sweaty/dirty/cold or being otherwise strained or inconvenienced physically (unless it's in the name of a photo opportunity or part of a team-building exercise). At the top end of this class – investment bankers, CEOs, former prime ministers and their spouses – earnings will exceed anyone in the Upper Class, the Queen included. At the other end – shop assistants, office drones – earnings will be dwarfed by the income of everyone else. Probably educated to university level, often in a subject that has nothing to do with their job.

Working Class. Anyone who relies on trades, trading, and physical attributes to earn a crust. From professional footballers to plumbers, plus the short-term unemployed in these professions, with incomes that frequently trump those of the Middle or Upper Classes. Also anyone who still believes that the old class model remains unchanged.

Underclass. Anyone who's long-term unemployed, on benefits, working in the black market, or engaged in criminal activity. Embracing everyone from benefit cheats to asylum seekers, the Underclass have no money and little influence, yet they are frequently cited by politicians, the media, and everyone above them in the system as the cause of all that's wrong in the UK.

In all cases, the things to avoid when it comes to class are the same as they ever were – never misrepresent your own class, and beware misreading that of others.

COAST

Britain has a lot of coastline – more than 7000 miles of it. Around sixty per cent of it forms the coast of mainland Scotland, and its 790 outlying islands.

Anyone who's looking to do more than just admire the Atlantic and North Sea from the cliff-tops will find they are not alone in their desire to dip a toe in the water. Like much of northern Europe, Britain has its fair share of open water swimmers who are determined to pursue their passion throughout the year, however icy the water.

The daily mantra of these single-minded individuals – that 'the sea is there to be swum in, and must be conquered' – is one that is frequently adopted by any Brits on holiday in the UK. Well, for the first day of the holiday, anyway.

COCAINE

Named by the NHS in late 2009 as the 'drug of choice for under-25s'. Cocaine (and its legion of nicknames, *Charlie*, *Gak*, and *Snow* among them) was once the drug of choice in the City of the 1980s, mainly due to its expense and associated elitism.

In recent years, the price (and quality) has fallen as the availability has risen. While the efforts of various drug enforcement agencies have resulted in an estimated drop in usage, the UN's 2009 report still found the UK to have more users than anywhere else in Europe – around one million, 860,000 of them in England alone.

COCKNEY

Being born and bred in London once granted you the right to award yourself this label, providing you were born within earshot of the church-bells at Bow. The primary privilege this afforded you has been the use of a bizarre vernacular – cockney rhyming slang.

This creative, amusing, but frankly somewhat time-consuming system replaces simple words such as 'stairs' and 'tea' with similar sounding mouthfuls – 'apples and pears' and 'Rosie Lee' respectively. Even more confusingly, sections of the phrase are often dropped – usually that part of the phrase which provides the rhyme.

So, 'Posh and Becks' (sex) will be shortened for convenience to 'Posh'. Much of East London would be largely unintelligible, then, were it not for the fact that rhyming slang is hardly heard any more.

That is, apart from by the 'mockneys', who affect the slang and the dropped consonants of the cockney accent. Whether they do this to sound cool, be served quicker in pubs, or to get some Posh, is not particularly crystal.

COFFEE

Britain's love affair with hot drinks has flip-flopped between tea and coffee over the last few centuries. The proliferation of coffee shops on the UK's high street is not a fad that began in the late 1990s – the first wave began in 1650, with the opening of the 'first coffeehouse in Christendom', in Oxford.

Coffeehouses were instrumental in the popularisation of tea, as the influence of the East India Company rose from 1654. Until the Cafe-Costa-Bucks franchise explosion, the UK was largely seen as a coffee-bean philistine by visitors to these shores – though Britain still leads Europe in its consumption of instant coffee.

It also remains a popular proving ground for an industry looking to test products, from self-heating cans of instant granules, to variants flavoured with Turkish Delight and Tia Maria. Whether this under-lines the UK consumers' reputation for adventurousness, or simply suggests unbelievable bad taste, is impossible to say.

Colonies

In the days when the sun never set on the British Empire, it was considered acceptable behaviour for European forces to turn up anywhere in the 'new' world and declare it part of their realm. Though it was generally unwise to do so without the manpower and firepower that would back up such a claim.

By the time the 1949 Geneva Convention effectively outlawed such behaviour, Britain had already lost or relinquished control of most of its former colonies. The first to go were the thirteen colonies of the US in 1783 – though many of them had by that time joined the former colonies club, the Commonwealth.

For this reason the word 'colony', even prefixed by the word 'former', is only ever heard in a historical context. Not only is it demeaning to both a country's past and its independence, it tends to make a Brit adopt a shameful, hang-dog look, while staring at the ground. And rightly so.

Compliments

Whether out of insecurity, a need to be polite, self-effacing, and modest, or simply because they hate being the centre of attention, British people are notoriously bad at taking compliments.

The natural reaction seems to be a compulsion to return the compliment, and deflect attention away:

'You're look wonderful.'

'Really? I don't feel it! I didn't get much sleep last night.'

'No, you do.'

'Now *you're* looking *fantastic*. Did you get your hair cut?'

'No.'

'Oh. Well it really suits you.'

Condiments

If you're invited to someone's house, and you don't arrive at a mealtime, go to the kitchen. If the table is set with salt, pepper, vinegar, tomato ketchup *and* brown sauce, then you have truly arrived in Britain.

CONSERVATIVE PARTY

William Pitt the Younger may have laid down the basic principles of the Conservative political philosophy during his two tenures as prime minister, but he didn't call himself a 'Conservative'.

He also avoided the colloquial term 'Tory' – largely due to the value placed on independence in the eighteenth-century political arena. Though the term's roots in the Irish word for a cattle thief might have had something to do with his reluctance.

Pitt's intense patriotism and pragmatic approach laid the foundations for the party that became known as the Conservatives in the 1830s, under Robert Peel. Today the Conservatives retain their reputation for low taxation, a robust foreign policy, and limited government.

A recent shift of both major UK parties to the political centre has made spotting the differences between them a challenge for even the most interested members of the electorate. Although they seemed to fare poorly in the run-up to the 2010 elections, the coalition that resulted placed a fighting-fit Conservative Party half-back in power after thirteen years. Regardless of policies, for many the Conservative Party will always be the party of 'the establishment' – and its history and cultural links have provided valuable political ammunition to its opponents.

CONVERSATION

British conversations come in two main flavours – the everyday and the intimate. Everyday conversations are had with acquaintances and colleagues to 'pass the time of day' and will doubtless include the following topics:

- the weather
- each other's health (but headlines only)

- the health of each other's family (omitting any embarrassing details)
- brief details of how work is going
- potential holiday destinations
All other topics are considered beyond the pale of small-talk.

It is possible for these acquaintances and colleagues to advance their status to that of 'close friends and family'. Then, the allowed conversational topics can include:

- money worries
- who to vote for

- the behaviour of 'that neighbour next door'
  But only once tea or alcohol is involved.

CORONATION STREET

First broadcast – live – in 1960, *Corrie* is one of two soap operas to have consistently dominated the TV ratings in the last twenty years. It can still lay legitimate claim to dealing with the issues of the day, but it's not averse to occasionally stretching credibility with an audience-grabbing stunt – HRH Prince Charles and Brit rock band Status Quo have made notable cameo appearances (as themselves).

The show can also boast a Who's Who of former cast members, ranging from actors on the rise who appeared in early episodes (Sir Ben Kingsley, Martin Shaw, Prunella Scales) to established stars who have relished the chance to visit the street (Sir Ian McKellen, Peter Kay). Regarded with affection even by Brits who don't watch it, *Coronation Street*'s success is built on a generally broadly comic, upbeat tone – a claim that cannot be made by its chief ratings rival, *Eastenders*.

COUGHING

Brits have two approaches to coughing. Either they use it as thinking time:

'So, will you marry me?'
'(cough) ... well ...'

Or it is something they are utterly unable to stop, particularly when at a wedding, in a theatre, in a church, or in the middle of a moment of respectful silence.

Nothing is more annoying to a Brit than someone having the indecency to cough inconsiderately. The traditional British remedy for an outburst of coughing is silently seething, and occasionally, when it really won't do, glaring. In theory, water could be offered, as long as it is served with the required reproachful glare.

Unless you are, in fact, proposing marriage. In which case it might be time to leave.

COWES WEEK

At the end of July, the Isle of Wight prepares itself for the arrival of boats and crews from around the world, for the world's longest-running sailing regatta.

A fixture in the society calendar since 1826, the Cowes week daily schedule is packed with international-standard racing – in 2005 there were 1036 boats entered into events.

Anyone with a love of boats, the sea, or very posh accents is guaranteed to have a good time here, while the tides in the Solent north of the island provide a challenge for even the most able of seamen (and women).

CREAM TEA

The idea of a mid-afternoon offering of sandwiches, scones, jam, and clotted cream has been credited to Benedictine monks in Tavistock, West Devon, in the eleventh century.

Since the historians who did the attributing were also from Tavistock, it's possible that a bias may have crept in, so there's still scope for further investigation.

However, Britain's best cream teas are undoubtedly served in the south-west, though recipes will vary depending on whether you're in Dorset, Cornwall, or Devon. Afternoon tea in this style is also served in the UK's more upmarket hotels. Usually for around £1 million per person.

CRICKET

A sport that fills vast periods of time with equally vast amounts of posturing, pottering around, and stopping for a cup of tea was always going to be popular with the English. The first records of cricket in England date back to 1598, and by 1611 it had become so popular that devotees were being arrested for skipping church to play.

Despite a rule-book so arcane that Dan Brown would have trouble making it accessible, the rest of the planet started to catch on. In 1882

England was beaten, in England, for the first time by Australia, and the death of English cricket was pronounced. In the same moment, the long-running Ashes series was born, and the sport opened up to the world, even making an appearance at the 1900 Olympics.

While largely still an English obsession, Scotland has enjoyed success, winning the inaugural ICC Intercontinental Cup in 2004, and the sport is played across the length and breadth of Britain at every level.

And if anyone out there can write a single one of the rules onto a postage stamp, we'd be mightily impressed.

'CUDDLY'

Almost half of Britain's men and a third of its women are overweight, and the obesity rate is on a continuing upward spiral. It's little wonder, then, that the language has shifted, embracing the changing body-shape of the populace.

While its verb form '(getting) cuddly' implies frisky behaviour, if used as an adjective, it suggests that the person being described has ample enough flesh to provide a truly immersive hug.

And as such, is unlikely to be flattered by the observation.

CURRY

Curry houses have been a feature on the streets of the UK since 1810, when the pioneering Sake Dean Mohamed opened the Hindoostane Coffee House in London's George Street.

In keeping with his original concept, most menus feature dishes that have been created or significantly adapted for the British palate, so the creamy Korma favourite bears very little resemblance to its Indian original.

The curry that's widely touted as the UK's most popular meal, the Chicken Tikka Masala, isn't Indian at all – it's a creation of Bangladeshi restaurateurs, based in Britain.

CUSTOMS AND EXCISE

Merging the Inland Revenue (the taxman) with Her Majesty's Customs and Excise (the people who rummage around in your holiday luggage at the airport) was sold to the British public as a cost-saving exercise.

However, most Brits have quickly come to the conclusion it was simply a cunning plan – secretly agreed by the major political parties – to create a department so universally despised that it would actually make you feel better about the government itself.

It worked.

CVs

Once viewed as suspiciously self-congratulatory, the Curriculum Vitae is now at the heart of a (largely mistaken) belief that the class system is dead, the old boy network has disbanded, and meritocracy has finally arrived.

While everyone from management consultants to McDonalds trainees have at least three different versions of their career, legislation on age discrimination means it's no longer necessary for you to include your date of birth, nor is a photograph required. Bare-faced lying seems to be actively encouraged, while just directing someone to your Facebook page probably won't cut it.

 **D**

DATING

British people have a rather singular attitude to dating, distinct from the US, where after a date with someone it's fairly normal to either:

(a)   never to see each other again, or

(b)   wait until the second, or even third date, before deciding whether you want to pursue the burgeoning relationship.

Brits, however, have a tendency to:

(a)   dive in head-long straight away, or
(b)   avoid any possible awkwardness by spending the rest of their lives together.

Speed-dating is a relatively recent import to the UK. After decades of couples meeting drunkenly through friends (or more properly, in bed and hung over the next morning), the formality of such an imposed encounter meant speed-dating never really took off.

In recent years, online dating has become more mainstream (and much less 'geeky'). The privacy of dating via a home computer has satisfied the desire to meet like-minded Brits, in a sober, civilised, controlled, and slightly less intense way.

And *then* get drunk.

DEVOLUTION

Labour was elected to government in 1997 with the devolution of power a key promise in its manifesto. While it has largely kept to its pledges, the results have been mixed at best. Scotland, Wales, and Northern Ireland have now all had their own parliaments since 1998. England hasn't, for reasons no one really understands and no one in power is keen to explain.

Plans for a new elected regional assembly for the north-east were abandoned in 2004 after seventy-eight per cent of voters in the region rejected government proposals for the forum.

Even where devolution has succeeded for the most part (Scotland), there have been what might politely be described as 'hiccups'. Holyrood, the newly created parliament building, was finished behind schedule and at a cost of seven times its original £62 million budget.

Which proves Scotland was entirely capable of governing itself to the same standard as Whitehall.

DIETING

The rising levels of obesity in Britain led to an alarming possible solution in 2007. Fire chiefs in Lancashire were seriously considering charging a levy for assistance in leaving a home on anyone weighing more than 191kg.

Exactly how many people in the UK are on a diet at any given time is unknown, as it's a subject the already reticent Brits are understandably even less willing to discuss than salaries. But with the diet industry valued at around £10 billion in 2008, someone's clearly at it.

Generally speaking, the approach seems to involve replacing two meals a day with milkshakes or cereal bars. The more cynically minded might term this 'starvation', and braver individuals might call it 'useless'.

DISCOUNTS

The art of haggling, bartering, or otherwise getting a few pounds knocked off whatever you're buying has seen an increase in Britain.

Once considered bad form – politeness and discussions of money never being a particularly good combination in striking a deal – in 2009 *Which? Magazine* found that eighty-five per cent of its readers had successfully tried to get a discount on the high street.

One respondent was able to secure a £3700 knockdown on the price of a new kitchen, but we're miles away from the haggling seen in Morocco or India. Probably best tried at a market rather than the opera.

DIVIDING (PAYING) THE BILL

'Going Dutch' is the source of much consternation at the end of a meal in the UK, as the urge to pay as little as possible collides with the eternal desire to be polite. Combine this with the British reluctance to talk about money in general, and at some point it's inevitable that a calculator will be produced, and exact amounts worked out on a napkin.

Evenly splitting the bill is rarely satisfactory, as silent grimaces and mutterings from those who 'only had a starter' or 'one glass of wine' will begin to drift through the restaurant.

Inevitably, exasperation ensues as an enjoyable evening descends into a group tax return. Such circumstances are usually ended by those good enough to reach into their pockets for a second time, solving the problem by throwing money at it, rather than by shaming the reluctant non-payers.

Doctor Who

The longest running science fiction show in history, and a nearly permanent fixture in British TV schedules from 1963. The Doctor's temporary departure from the small screen in 1989 did little to dampen public affection for him.

The show ambitiously attempted to depict both the furthest flung corners of the universe, and their exotic (and largely hostile) residents, on a budget of about fifty quid a week. It epitomised the make-do-and-mend approach at the heart of the British character, while the Doctor reflected our knack for being eccentrically resourceful.

The Doctor's successful return in 2006 reinforced his appeal as a uniquely British hero, while the show's base in Cardiff gave the BBC a chance to bolster its commitment to expanding a regional production roster.

With more than 750 episodes behind him – including many early stories that were lost when the BBC destroyed the tapes – the regenerating Timelord is as popular as ever, and actually seems to be getting younger.

Matt Smith became the eleventh incarnation of the Doctor aged a mere twenty-seven, less than half the age of William Hartnell when he became the first actor in the role.

Double Deckers

One of the quintessential images of Britain, the two-decked 'Routemaster Omnibus' has been on UK roads since 1956.

The articulated single-deck 'bendy buses' introduced in 1981 made many Brits more nostalgic than ever for the old Routemaster, especially in London. In 2008 the newly elected mayor of London succumbed to the many public complaints and pledged to scrap the bendy bus.

Accessibility considerations mean that the double decker may not be returning to the fleet in its original design, though many old models are still in operation. Since Cliff Richard transformed one in the 1963 film *Summer Holiday* (famously installing a shower cubicle), double deckers have been used on Heritage routes and for private hire – whether you want to get married on one or charity drive it to Johannesburg.

The Routemaster Association is dedicated to preserving both the condition of remaining models and their iconic status overall. It may be up there with the red phone box for establishing shots in films, but bless us, we are a nostalgic lot.

DRESS DOWN FRIDAYS

The mid-1990s arrival of this US-imported practice coincided with a general relaxation of business dress codes in the UK. Unfortunately, for many Brits this meant that for one day a week even *more* effort was required in choosing what to wear.

A 2010 survey of London office workers found that Dress Down Fridays – along with other meaningless perks such as 'Employee of the Month' – were among the most cited causes of irritation at work.

DROUGHT

Despite its reputation for being a rainy place, the UK has actually been in a state of almost permanent drought since 1976, when a record-breaking heat-wave emptied many reservoirs.

Unsurprisingly, the continued drought hasn't always been due to sweltering summers – the hosepipe bans of 2005/06 were introduced as the result of the reservoirs being depleted by dry winters.

Regular seasonal warnings have had sadly little impact on the British, who, in comparison with much of the rest of the world, remain typically careless with water and still leave taps running for the laziest of reasons.

DUKE OF EDINBURGH

For reasons clear to pretty much no one, those achieving royal rank by marriage sometimes take the name of their well-connected spouse (as with Princess Michael of Kent).

Sometimes they don't, and the most famous example is Queen Elizabeth II's partner of more than fifty years, who is not referred to as 'king'.

Since being labelled the Royal Consort sounds a little demeaning, Phillip was given the title Duke of Edinburgh (conveniently created the night before by George VI, his father-in-law) on his wedding day in 1947.

He did enough good work to be promoted to the rank of Prince of the United Kingdom some ten years later, and has since lent his Duke title to a popular award scheme for young people, of which he is the founder.

DUNKING

Once a form of punishment performed with a ducking stool, dunking is now the sole preserve of anyone in possession of a biscuit and a cup of tea (or other hot drink).

Like even the most minority of interests in the UK, there are numerous societies dedicated to preserving and promoting this practice. The Biscuit Appreciation Society offers detailed advice for concerned users on avoiding disintegration, ideal vessel size, and recommended biscuit brands. Its key piece of advice is to avoid supermarkets' own imitations of established biscuit brands, as there are consistency problems.

By contrast, the savoury alternative of dunking bread in a bowl of soup is not good dining etiquette, and is universally frowned upon.

Which is a shame, as it's possibly even more delicious an activity than tea-dunking, especially because it's frowned upon.

~~ ❉ **E** ❉ ~~

EASTENDERS

While many once criticised the BBC's decision to commission a twice-weekly soap opera, the show has been an undoubted success, dominating the ratings since its first transmission in 1985.

Dirty Den's Christmas Day divorce attracted more than thirty million viewers in the UK in 1986, though the show's popularity did dip in the mid-noughties, with just four million in 2007 tuning in to see a car crash that constituted the show's most expensive stunt ever.

Regardless of audience share, *Eastenders* has never shied from addressing major issues of the day. In contrast with its Mancunian rival *Coronation Street*, the East End storylines involve physical and verbal abuse, at the very least. The show has a long list of complainants and critics, from the Metropolitan Police to the *Daily Mail* who feel they – or issues that concern them – have been misrepresented.

Though it's fair to say the show's producers aren't averse to a bit of misrepresentation. Despite its name – and the substitution of Bromley-By-Bow for 'Walford East' on the show's Underground map – the *Eastenders* characters go about their day's graft on the BBC's Elstree Borehamwood studios (located in the genteel extremities of London's north-west suburbs).

ECSTASY

MDMA was *the* UK drug of the 1990s and helped shape our nascent rave culture. Its popularity exploded with Manchester's music scene – especially at the Hacienda Club, whose demise is often attributed to the owners never being able to sell enough alcohol to its permanently tripping patrons.

First synthesised in 1912, it was assigned the code name EA-1475 by the CIA, who experimented with its use in their MK Ultra research into brainwashing and mind control in the 1950s.

Presumably they had an OK time with the drug, as it remained legal in the US until 1984. By that point it had already been illegal in the UK for seven years, and was taking off in the gay clubs of Dallas under the alias Adam.

It acquired its most widely used name in the late 1980s, along with a neat marketing gimmick – designs stamped on the pills, from the Superman symbol to a smiley face.

Usage had waned by 2003, along with the end of the rave scene, when the number of users had fallen by twenty per cent. In terms of youth popularity, it has largely been replaced by cocaine.

EDEN PROJECT (THE)

One of the National Lottery Funding Project's success stories, this state-of-the-art greenhouse sunk into a 60m crater is home to 130,000 plants and more than 3500 different species.

The success of the attraction since its opening in 2001 has been both critical and commercial; botanists and biologists rave about the educational benefits, while immense (but good natured) queues make it among the UK's most popular attractions – in 2009 it welcomed its ten millionth visitor.

If that isn't reason enough for heading to Cornwall, the toilets won the 2003 award for Best Loo in Britain.

EDINBURGH

Aberdeen may be older, Glasgow may be bigger, but Edinburgh earns its right to be Scotland's capital by punching its cultural weight, and then some.

Throw in some staggering architecture, and you get quite a capital.

The defensive walls that surrounded the city meant that with space at a premium, residents without the means to live in one of Edinburgh's pioneering high-rise buildings were forced to dig. The remains of the makeshift underground metropolis they fashioned can still be toured today.

Renowned for its literary history, Edinburgh has more booksellers per head of population than anywhere else in Britain, and its annual International Book Festival in August has been an important date in the artistic calendar since 1947. In terms of eye-catching impact, books are now shaded out by theatre, in the form of the Edinburgh Festival Fringe. Fringe audiences can catch everything from the most controversial stand-up comedy acts to Shakespeare (as performed by tiny ninja puppets). Anyone uncertain of what to see can be entertained simply by standing on Princes Street, and watching the wacky world go by.

Away from festival time, the city goes equally crazy for Hogmanay, the Scottish New Year celebrations. The cliff-top castle (part of which dates back to the twelfth century) provides a dramatic backdrop to the midnight firework displays, and at its feet an annual street party is held (which drew 80,000 people in 2009).

EISTEDDFOD

Pronounced eye-STETH-fod, the National Eisteddfod of Wales is an annual festival of literature, music, and performance, which can be traced back to the twelfth century. In its modern form since 1880, it is now strongly linked to the movement to keep the Welsh language alive and thriving. As a move to promote the international appeal of the festival, many shopkeepers in Llangollen accept the euro as payment for its duration.

The Youth Eisteddfod (Eisteddford yr Urdd) has certainly succeeded in making as broad an appeal as possible. The Urdd is now the largest festival of its kind in Europe, regularly attracting over 15,000 competitors.

48

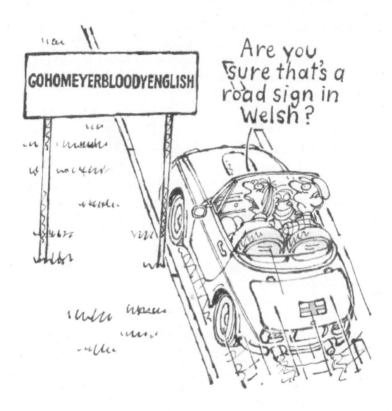

'ELEPHANT IN THE ROOM'

As well as providing the graffiti artist Banksy with the inspiration for his 2006 show *Barely Legal*, this phrase is of particular importance to the British. Our ability to avoid issues is infamous.

The term is often applied to political topics which may be discussed, even hotly debated, in private – the troubles in Northern Ireland, population growth, immigration – but about which in public, politicians will offer only the most meaningless of platitudes.

It can equally apply to domestic matters – privately held beliefs that it would be utterly inappropriate to mention (the age difference between friends and their new partners, or the style and/or design of an item of clothing worn at a family gathering).

Where more than two Brits are gathered together, it's safe to say there'll be an elephant lumbering about too.

EMANCIPATION

In the USA, Lincoln used the Emancipation Proclamation to free all slaves currently in rebellion. In Britain, emancipation is more associated with the political activist Emmeline Pankhurst, the leader of the suffragette movement. Pankhurst was instrumental in the fight for a woman's right to be educated, to work, and to vote – essentially, the right to be treated equally with men.

The campaign reached most people's awareness when the suffragette Emily Davison was trampled to death by one of the king's horses at Epsom Derby in 1913.

Women were granted equal voting rights on 2 July 1928, though Pankhurst did not live to see her dream achieved – she had died nineteen days previously, aged sixty-nine. In 1930 a statue was unveiled in Westminster to commemorate her life and achievements.

EMIGRATION

While Great Britain has traditionally been a net importer of citizens, in recent years it has also been losing Brits at a faster rate than ever before.

The Office of National Statistics showed that more than 427,000 Brits left the UK in 2008, with the sunnier climes, more spacious surroundings, and cheerier soap operas of Australia and New Zealand attracting thirty-two per cent of them.

The fact that the figures show record-breaking departures might be a cause for concern, if it weren't for the fact that the records in question only date back as far as 1991.

'ENCHANTED'

An extremely polite and complimentary alternative to the more familiar greeting of 'Pleased to meet you'. While it can often be used to devastating effect by speakers with the slightest trace of a non-UK accent, it should be used sparingly by Brits, if at all.

ENGLISH PLACE-NAME SOCIETY (EPNS)

Founded in 1923 to carry out the Survey of English Place-Names, the society began publishing its annual report on the origins, development, and distribution of names in 1969.

With admirable British reserve, the society applies the same analytical rigour in all its labours, even when confronted by place-names as patently absurd as Brown Tongue, Bell End, Great Cockup, and Lickey Hole.

ENID BLYTON

The enduring popularity of this author of over 600 books is in defiance of all things politically correct. The Golliwog character, while an entirely benign and lovable presence in Toytown, is hardly in step with contemporary attitudes; and the exclusively white, middle-class characters of her teen adventures contributed to her falling seriously out of fashion from the 1960s onwards.

However, for many, her books represent a nostalgic view of Britain when children had seemingly little to fear and everything to explore. By UNESCO's estimations she is the fifth most translated writer in history, and anyone who once read her stories will still know how to get out of a locked room (as long as the key is in the door on the other side).

ENTENTE CORDIALE

The fraught nature of the relationships between European nations in the early twentieth century even has its own boardgame, *Diplomacy*. In 1904 alliances and agreements criss-crossed the map of Europe and Asia like the tangled web of a special-needs spider.

Nonetheless, the decision taken by the UK and France to ignore their respective allies and not fight each other in the Russo-Japanese War still seems remarkable. The understandings they reached that year – a union that stopped just short of guaranteeing military support – formed the foundation for the (relatively) strong links we enjoy today.

EQUALITY

Equality of employment and rights in the UK is protected by assorted legislation, notably the Sex Discrimination Act (1975), the Race Relations Act (1976), and the Equality Act (2006).

How free of discrimination this legislation has made British society is impossible to say, but it's certainly been a gold mine for the lawyers. Regardless of age, race, sex, disability, religion, gender reassignment, or sexual orientation, you are guaranteed a fair hearing in the offices of any number of well-heeled solicitors.

The groups who still feel discriminated against include those with red hair (the regular butt of jokes) and middle-aged white men (who were feeling left out).

ESSEX

A county near London, unfairly renowned for being predominantly populated by wide-boy men and women of questionable morals, thanks to a preponderance of jokes made about them in the latter half of the twentieth century.

In 2010, the Essex Women's Advisory Group succeeded in raising £38,000 to counteract the stereotype by highlighting the success of local figures such as author Jilly Cooper and actress Maggie Smith.

While these good intentions may sell more books and DVDs, it's sadly unlikely to curb the jokes.

ESTATES

If you hear people saying they 'live on an estate', it can mean one of two things. Either they live in the middle of the country in a mansion surrounded by lots of private land, and are probably on first-name terms with the Queen, or (more likely) they live in one of the UK's three million council properties.

As the country estate began its great decline during World War I, the first wave of council housing construction came as the result of Prime Minister David Lloyd George's 'homes for heroes' initiative. By the onset of World War II, the proportion of public vs private housing in the UK had gone up from 1 per cent to 10 per cent. Homes were built to high specifications, with gardens and large rooms.

Growing demand led to an unfortunate relaxing of standards in the 1950s. Construction schedules of almost 450,000 new homes a year were met, and by 1979 nearly half the British population lived in council housing.

The deterioration of existing properties and negative associations attached to council estates means that, like the country estate, they are in decline, albeit for wholly different reasons.

ETON

Founded in 1440, attended by nineteen British prime ministers (and largely responsible for the notion that British men have a love of being spanked), Eton's original mission was the education of seventy poor boys, prior to their attendance at Cambridge University.

These 'King's Scholars' now represent just a fraction of the pupil population of 1300, though the Cambridge link of the past remains – thirty per cent of students go on to study either there or at Oxford.

For those not lucky enough to win one of the seventy scholarships, the school currently charges just under £30,000 a year to attend, in return for which, you'll guarantee your child a first-class education, and the likelihood of being written off as an upper-class snob by anyone still looking to invoke a misguided class war.

EUROPE

Britain's relationship with Europe is the kind beloved by gossip magazines – always turbulent, frequently affectionate, and certainly never dull. Even Brits who talk about Europe in positive terms will refer to it as if it were somewhere far, far away.

And with good reason – the rest of Europe does things that Britain can only aspire to. Most Europeans are bilingual, have a singular cuisine they can boast about, get to use well-run public transportation systems, and manage to maintain a healthy distance in their relationship with the USA.

As a result, the British always do their best to hide their feelings when talking about other parts of Europe, since every single country Over There seems to do at least one thing significantly better than the UK.

Apart from Poland, which does everything to the same standard as the UK, but for an eighth of the cost.

EXCHEQUER

The medieval name for the office charged with collecting revenue from the people. It's more likely, though, that the chancellor of that institution will be cited as the man responsible for any economic woes you may be experiencing, rather than the office itself – especially since the government department supporting that chancellor is the treasury, not the exchequer. Confused? Well, it seems, so are they, most of the time.

Despite the gravity of the responsibilities that come with the office, successive chancellors have not been averse to a bit of fun, especially on budget day. The tradition of posing for the press with the battered red box dates back to 1869, when George Ward Hunt arrived at the

House of Commons to find he'd left it – and his speech – at home. Ever since, it is clearly shown.

The chancellor also enjoys the unique privilege of being allowed alcohol during the delivery of his speech. The longest serving chancellor in modern times, Gordon Brown, is thought never to have taken advantage of this benefit, though he did ask for a new box to replace the nineteenth-century antique he inherited.

The new red box was made by dockyard trainees in Brown's own constituency (presumably in a bid to deliver some localised fiscal stimulus).

Excuses

We seem to view excuses with the same contempt as Rudyard Kipling, who once said 'We have forty million reasons for failure, but not a single excuse.'

It may all be very subjective, but for a Brit a reason is always genuine, and an excuse always lame. Examples abound in the archives of the TV Licensing Authority. Among its list of worst excuses in 2009 for not buying a £142.50 licence are:

- 'My dog watches the telly while I'm at work to keep him company – not me.'
- 'I couldn't make my last payment as my baby was sick on my shoulder and I didn't want to go to the shop smelling of sick because the guy I fancy works there.'

And finally:

- 'My husband has just spent £3000 on this massive flat-screen digital TV, so we can't possibly afford a licence.'

Which, you have to admit, is a pretty good reason.

~~ ❋ **F** ❋ ~~

Famous British Heroes

In 2002, a BBC poll of the 100 most famous Britons threw up a few surprises, a number of predictably familiar names and faces, and several issues.

While avoiding some of the most common gaffes – such as including Bono, an Irish citizen – a considerable number of those featured on the list would not have considered themselves British, or possibly not even known what was meant by the term.

Famous 'Brit hero' Richard the Lionheart went off on the crusades sporting the *English* cross of St George (and he generally lived in France). 'Brit hero' Owain Glyndwr fought the English for Welsh sovereignty, as William Wallace did for the Scots. And 'Brit hero' Arthur was the only king who might well have embraced the notion of 'Britain', but he probably didn't exist.

The one figure on the list to famously and openly embrace all things British and regularly appear wearing the Union Jack is Freddie Mercury. Who was born in Zanzibar and raised in India.

FAREWELL

An olde, fond way to say *goodbye*, from 'fare thee well'. Farewell has largely fallen out of use in the UK, along with *forsooth* ('for see the truth'), *yonder* ('here and yon') and *gosh* ('god and shhh'). *Welcome*, from 'you are well come' is still in use, though the olde version sounds cosier.

FAUX PAS

Literally, the French for 'false step', and used in British society to describe something that has been said or done which is considered to be utterly socially inappropriate:

'In retrospect, I think sleeping with her mother was something of a faux pas.'

FENG SHUI

A term the British use on a regular basis, with little sense of its key principles or 2000-year history.

'What's happened to my footrest?'

'It's in the shed.'

'What's it doing there?'

'It didn't look right in the lounge ... it was bad feng shui.'

No commission has studied which words and terms cause the greatest number of arguments between couples in the UK. When someone finally does get round to it, expect to find this in the top ten.

'FINE'

If you ask Brits how they are, and they reply *fine*, you can assume two things:

1) They are responding in the appropriate manner for such a question.
2) They are, actually, anything but 'fine'.

This presents a dilemma.

Should you pursue the matter, and continue questioning until you discover what's wrong?

Or do you adhere to the tacit agreement which states that an enquiry into well-being is purely small-talk and shouldn't encourage genuine answers?

Either way, the likely result will be:

'No, really, how are you?'

'No, *really*, I'm fine.'

At which point you should probably start to worry.

FIRE BRIGADE

Universally loved today, even during periods of industrial action, the UK Fire Service had a surprisingly mercenary origin. Set up in the aftermath of the Great Fire of London in 1666, brigades were the brainchild of the city's insurance companies. As a result, they were instructed to only fight fires in insured buildings, identified by external markings.

Now we have over 35,000 brave individuals whose job is to routinely walk into buildings that are on fire. It makes sitting at a keyboard seem slightly less heroic.

FIRST CLASS VS POSH

The name for the fastest (and most expensive) standard service provided by Royal Mail, the most spacious (and expensive) train carriages you can travel in, and the highest level of academic degree attainable (which may not be that expensive, but is certainly hard work). Anything *excellent*, then, is *first class*.

Posh was thought to have its roots in a similar classification. The story goes that upmarket travellers on cruisers bound for India in the days of the Raj wanted to be berthed in the shade for the majority of their voyage. To this end, they would change cabins for each leg of the journey voyage – so Port Out, Starboard Home. Unfortunately, there's no surviving evidence that this was the case.

The adjective *posh* is certainly not interchangeable with *first class*. And with all due respect to Mrs David Beckham, and the players and supporters of Peterborough United FC, it tends to be mildly derogatory.

FISH'N'CHIPS

A chippy is a carpenter. *The* chippy is where you go for a fish fillet fried in batter and thickly cut chips doused in salt and vinegar, to be eaten out of paper (that's been free of newsprint by law since 1980). Or that's where you go if you can still find a plaice that's devoted to the dish.

While fish and chips remains on the menu throughout the UK, it is just one offering on a sliding scale of alternatives ranging far beyond the traditional saveloy sausages, ever-popular mushy peas, and the calorific deep-fried Mars Bar.

Environmental and cost concerns recently hit supplies of cod and it seemed the public had haddock enough. In 2009 the fish supper was beaten into fifth place for the title of 'most consumed takeaway', after burgers, Chinese/Indian, fried chicken and pizza.

Flags

While they remain a sensitive and often divisive issue in Northern Ireland, a general suspicion of flags and their associations with political violence seemed to be overcome in the 1990s.

The devolution of power to Wales and Scotland, begun in 1997, has helped lead to a surge in the appearance of the Welsh Red Dragon and Scottish Cross of St Andrew.

The increased usage of both, particularly on government buildings, has been a source of satisfaction for those who view the Union Jack as a 'butcher's apron', symbolic of English oppression.

The English Cross of St George has been more prominently associated in marketing England's football team since 2002, and is most visible hanging from vehicles and in residential windows during international tournaments. As a symbol, it struggles to shake its negative associations with the far right.

As the poet John Agard says:

> 'What's that, fluttering in the breeze?
> It's just a piece of cloth,
> That brings a nation to its knees.'

Football

While rugby, cricket, and Gaelic football attract sizable crowds at every level they are played, regular football is the most popular sport in the UK. First mentioned in records from 1174, the Elizabethans called it 'the game of the gutter', and games in the 1930s attracted largely male crowds of up to 150,000. Unsurprisingly, these were boisterous affairs, with violence and hooliganism commonplace.

The Hillsborough disaster in 1989 forced a major rethink of the strategies deployed to deal with the nastier element that the game attracted, as the high pitch-perimeter fences designed to contain fans led to the deaths of ninety-six Liverpool supporters. Since Hillsborough, policing of games has shifted and club stadiums in the top divisions have become all-seater.

For many the loss of the old terraces has led to a gentrification of the game and a betrayal of its roots – though anyone of a sensitive nature might feel that the language on display both from the players and the audience makes for anything but a family affair.

Attempts to clean up this area of the game have met with mixed success. Successive campaigns against racism, including 'Kick it Out' in 1993, have helped make the chants heard less obviously racist, but they remain adult in content, industrial in language, and spiteful in tone.

In 2010 an attempt to prosecute a Millwall fan accused of racial abuse after calling a Gillingham player a 'pikey' was unsuccessful. Central to his defence was the fact that many Gillingham fans refer to themselves as 'pikeys' and wear T-shirts to matches proclaiming this very thing.

FREEMASONS (THE BROTHERHOOD)

A predominantly (traditionally completely) male 'society with secrets' that numbers around 400,000 UK members in 8000 lodges. Freemasonry is first mentioned in Scottish records dating back to 1599, with its first grand lodge established in England in 1717. An early export to the fledgling United States, it's estimated that there are now five million members meeting at lodges worldwide.

All of which makes rather strange the fact that no one outside the organisation seems any wiser now about the details of what goes on at meetings than we were 200 years ago.

Where high profile exposées have surfaced, their claims have tended to be dismissed as publicity-seeking hoaxes. The organisation has tried to address this, claiming that meetings are taken up with a combination of internal administration and lessons in the Craft.

The admission by Master Masons that initiation ceremonies only involve members rolling up their trouser legs has only served to further whet the appetite of conspiracy theorists.

Concern about the influence of 'the Brotherhood' – which claims to be the UK's largest secular, fraternal, and charitable organisation – led the Home Secretary Jack Straw to insist that all new judges and police officers should disclose their membership as of 1999. This requirement was quietly dropped in 2009.

So if the Masons are as influential in the UK as many claim, they're also a little slow off the mark when it comes to covering their tracks.

FUNERALS

The Welsh, Irish, and Scottish fine balance of the solemnity of such a gathering with a slightly more celebratory post-funeral 'wake' is one the English have increasingly picked up on.

The other key change in recent years in the UK has been a result of the growing waistline of the average Brit. In 2010 a new crematorium in the West Midlands – where twenty-six per cent of the population are classified as obese – was revealed to feature a 1.1m opening for bodies after the previous building's 90cm passageway was found inadequate for some of its larger occupants.

GAMBLING

The UK gambling industry has considerably improved its image since 1994, and the launch of the UK's national lottery. The appearance of bookmakers on the UK's high streets changed, with bright, open retail units replacing the seedy and secluded dens of old. The addition of flat-screen TVs and coffee machines suggest that perhaps you've wandered into a community centre.

There has been an overall growth in the numbers gambling in the UK, with 600,000 'problem' UK gamblers considered addicted in 2010, largely due to online gambling, particularly online poker.

The British also remain devoted to placing outrageous wagers on everything: betting on soap opera storylines, whether snow will fall at Christmas, or who will be cast next as Doctor Who.

Possibly the most outrageous bet ever made in the UK was in 1960, when a man bet £10 (at odds of 1000–1) that humans would walk on the moon before the decade was out. It turned out pretty well for him. At least it did until he died behind the wheel of the sports car he bought with his winnings.

GASTROPUBS

A mid-1990s phenomenon still apparent in the UK, often said to have started at The Eagle in London's Farringdon – which is *not* the same Eagle mentioned in 'Pop Goes the Weasel'.

Essentially, a regular pub which has spent a large quantity of money on a refurbishment, replacing wooden stools with comfortable chairs, glass tables with distressed timber, and carpets with a wooden floor.

Changing the food is deemed slightly less important than changing the wording on the menu. So the 'Hand-crafted Andalucian Chorizo with Pomme Purée' will closely resemble the 'Sausage and Mash' the same chef prepared for you before they refurbished. But you'll now be charged restaurant prices for it, largely to pay for all the new furniture.

'GEORDIE'

The nickname for people from the north-east of England (specifically Tyneside), and for their dialect, considered to be one of the hardest to imitate in the UK. Geordies have a reputation for being friendly and going out a lot, often while not wearing much clothing, even when it's minus eight outside.

GEORGIAN

The period of history when Kings George I, II, III, and IV reigned (1714–1830). Architecturally, known for richly designed interiors, and more reserved exteriors. Much like the British character.

GIBRALTAR

The Empire may well be a thing of the past, but Britain has retained a few of its outposts, particularly those in areas of strategic military importance. This has often annoyed neighbouring countries, and Spain's attitude to the two and a quarter square miles of Gibraltar has been no exception.

The Rock's tacky British themed pubs would make a walking tour of the Falklands a preferable holiday destination, and the UK government would surely rather offload the economic burden of maintaining it.

Given that the last referendum – in 1967 – of its inhabitants found that 99.6 per cent wanted to remain under UK control, it looks set to celebrate the three hundredth anniversary of being British in 2013.

GIFTS

It would be easy for any observer to assume that the British have a profound distaste for any form of gift. The presentation of even the most token of offerings will be accompanied by an extensive litany of reasons why the giver should not have pursued such a course of action.

Do not be fooled by this.

The British love receiving gifts as much as anyone, and will devote considerable time after any social gathering appraising the worth of the giver based on the value of the gift. The big three gift-giving occasions to be aware of are:

Dinner

If someone cooks dinner for you, take a bottle of wine. Do not spend less on the bottle than it cost you to get to their home, and do not keep the bottle next to you at the table for your own personal consumption. Or take it home with you, no matter what they say.

Moving house

If someone you know has recently moved and invites you over, bring a house-warming present in addition to your alcoholic offering. This should be a practical rather than a frivolous item, such as a cafetière, a spice rack, or a bread maker. Most Brits tend to give away items that they received the last time they moved house.

Christmas/Hanukkah/Winter Festive period

Being asked to spend any time with someone over the festive period between 24 December and 2 January is a big deal in Britain, but fortunately the rules that apply here are fairly universal. Try to bring gifts for any children you know will be present, ideally ones that don't require batteries or make any noise. Whatever else you bring, don't bother spending a lot of money on gifts for the parents of your partner. If they are going to like you, they'll do it of their own volition. Besides, any attempt to bribe your way into their affections will be irrelevant once the board-games come out.

Birthdays are conspicuous by their absence from this list, as no one in the UK has bothered with providing birthday gifts for anyone but their immediate family for decades, other than a drink. Or a last-minute over-priced 'comedy' card from the newsagent.

GILBERT AND SULLIVAN

The British love of decorative language, cross dressing, twee music, and double entendre all find a home outside pantomime, in the operettas of librettist William Gilbert and composer Arthur Sullivan.

While anyone new to their work may be appalled by the superficial and clearly xenophobic portrayal of other nationalities, the good news is that whatever the backdrop, their real targets are the British.

From the class-obsessed officers of their first major success *HMS Pinafore* (1878) to the petty officialdom of *The Mikado* (1885), G&S delighted in lampooning the very British institutions that had made the UK an all-powerful empire. And they managed all this despite a not particularly harmonious working relationship.

Asked about his collaborator's solo work, *Ivanhoe*, Gilbert remarked 'I expected to be bored, and I was not. That is the highest compliment I have ever paid a grand opera.' Gilbert had refused a complimentary seat, insisting on paying for his own ticket.

GIN (MOTHER'S RUIN)

By 1730, a glass of gin in the UK was cheaper than a glass of beer. Its potency, along with supposedly medicinal qualities, led to a surge in popularity, particularly among women.

Successive rafts of government licensing legislation from 1736 helped calm the craze, side-stepping the kind of general chaos depicted by Hogarth in the painting *Gin Lane*.

Rising grain prices also played a key role in curbing what may have become a social epidemic. It seems they've continued to rise – a gin and tonic can be sold for £12, which is a bit steep for sparkling alcohol.

GLAMOUR (PAGE 3) MODEL

The titillation of UK tabloid readers stepped up a gear on 17 November 1970, when German model Stephanie Rahn became the first to appear topless in the *Sun*. Since then, the Page 3 'feature' has spawned imitators, on page 5 of the *Mirror* and pretty much every page of the *Star*.

A topless model became a permanent feature at the *Sun* in 1975, and in 1988 spawned a sibling – the Page 7 Fella, who sadly made it only as far as his seventh birthday before being quietly shown the door.

GLASTONBURY

The Woodstock Music and Art Fair of 1969 predated Glasto by five years, but the Somerset devotees won't let a little thing like the Gregorian calendar stop them from referring to it as the founding rock of music festivals.

With around 177,000 ticketholders partying the weekend away, the atmosphere is as electric as the smell around the festival's toilet sites is overwhelming. Despite humble beginnings, a growing ticket price, and a reputation for chiming with the worst weather the British climate has to offer, Glastonbury continues to go from strength to strength.

Organisers Michael Eavis and (now) his daughter Emily have a knack for attracting captivating headline acts. But they've managed to do this while balancing the festival's diverse communities – from hip-hop hedonists to new-age healers – helping make the festival a much-admired fixture in Britain's summer calendar, especially by those who have never attended, and are among the sixteen million Brits to watch the mud-slinging and biblical downpours from the comfort of their own homes.

GOLF

While golf is largely a sport of the affluent in England and Wales, across Scotland and Northern Ireland it has a far broader following and a huge number of high-standard courses open to all. Indeed, Scotland is regularly cited as the birthplace of the game.

It became so popular they had to ban the game from 1457 to 1502 – it was proving too much of a distraction from preparing their defences against the attacking English.

While there are quality courses all over Britain, Rickmansworth arguably offers golfers their best chance of a hole-in-one. In 1960, Mrs Paddy Martin, playing off a handicap of 18, was able to achieve a hole-in-one on the 125-yard third hole three times in four days.

'GOLLIWOG'

The marketing gimmick for Robertson's – official purveyors of jam and marmalade to Her Majesty the Queen – first appeared in 1895 in the children's book *The Adventures of Two Dutch Dolls and a Golliwogg*.

A melancholy but friendly character, the black doll went on to earn considerable revenue for just about everyone involved with him. Everyone, that is, apart from Florence Kate Upton, the illustrator of the book he'd debuted in, as she hadn't trademarked her creation.

His later, more unpalatable roles (as a car thief in Enid Blyton's *Here Comes Noddy Again* in 1951) provided fuel for the debate on the racial stereotypes he represented. Appearances in either doll form or as a marketing icon from the 1960s onwards became increasingly rare.

The word retains an ugly flavour in the UK, and its reported use in 2009 by Carol Thatcher (the D-list media celebrity daughter of the former prime minister) served as a reminder both of the power and the history of its associations.

GOVERNMENT COMMUNICATION HEADQUARTERS (GCHQ)

The UK security services' doughnut-shaped chief listening post is located in the town of Cheltenham, and houses over 5000 staff. As well as intercepting and decoding intelligence transmissions across the globe (eavesdropping and snooping), staff at GCHQ also engage in 'fieldwork', when circumstances demand it.

In 2003 they led their own investigation into a series of daily, high-frequency broadcasts emanating from Yorkshire. The source was revealed to be a love-struck ram, attempting to mate with a radio mast, in Scarborough.

GREEN BELT

The idea of protecting an area of land from development or construction and curbing urban sprawl seemed fairly uncontroversial when it was implemented in the UK in 1955.

Around sixteen per cent of Northern Ireland is now designated as Green Belt; Wales has one large stretch between Newport and Cardiff; Scotland has seven Green Belt areas; and England more than a dozen, constituting thirteen per cent of its land.

GREEN PARTY

Born in the 1970s and known as the Ecology Party until 1985, a ballot paper marked for the 'Greens' used to be little more than a protest vote. Their commitment to responsible, environmental policy-making above all else has made them a single-issue party in the eyes of the UK electorate.

Success in Europe gave the alliance of Green parties more of a platform – they were able to record fifteen per cent of the overall vote in the 1989 European Elections. It's also made the big three parties keener than ever to get in on the action, and all have happily borrowed ideas from the Green manifesto.

While they've continued to see a rise in their share of the vote at all elections, they seem likely to remain a minority force within the UK although they gained their first MP in Brighton in 2010. Only when they manage to be implicated in expenses scandals in Brussels and Westminster can the Greens claim to have truly arrived as a major political party.

GREENWICH MEAN TIME

The maritime supremacy of the UK may be a distant memory now, but serving as the baseline for all world time zones is at least a link to former glories.

For most visitors to the Royal Observatory, the key reason for a trip is to pose for a picture while straddling the Prime Meridian, where the Eastern hemisphere meets the West. And very exciting it is too, although in truth Greenwich has had no less than four meridians running through it since 1675.

The 0° line marked out by a brass rail – known as Airey's Line – has been in use since 1851, and was adopted internationally by twenty-five countries in 1884. It's probably less important than the third meridian – Bradley's – whose line is now used by UK map-makers, despite being nearly six metres from Airey's Line in places (they positioned their measuring equipment in neighbouring rooms).

This detail – along with the fact that Co-ordinated Universal Time (as measured by atomic clocks) is now the key driver in time measurement – shouldn't get in the way of anyone enjoying a visit to the site. The views of London from the Observatory are terrific.

GREETINGS CARDS

While the greetings card had been around for centuries, the Brit Henry Cole – who founded the Victoria and Albert Museum – can lay claim to coming up with the world's first Christmas card.

Apparently tired of writing letters to people, he commissioned an artist in 1843 to design an illustration he could send in place of any actual correspondence. The card market in the UK is now worth over £1.7 billion annually, with an average of thirty-one cards being given by every person, forty-three per cent of them at Christmas.

Figures are sadly not available on what percentage of these cards had been purchased at petrol stations or all-night newsagents, or how many had been in their packaging for less than a minute before being opened, signed, sealed, and handed over.

GUINNESS

A pint of the black stuff might be Ireland's most recognised icon, but for most of the last century the UK has been Guinness' biggest market.

A batch of six barrels arrived in London in 1769, ten years after it became a central part of the diet of Dubliners. Its growth since then made the original St James Gate brewery the biggest on the planet by the start of the twentieth century.

While Arthur Guinness was renowned for never writing any of his recipes down, it's likely that the drink has undergone a transformation over the years from ale, to porter, to the stout we know today – the key shift coming with the addition of roasted barley, which gave the drink its characteristic colour and rich sweetness.

Marketed as 'Good for you', its apparent health benefits and meal-in-a-glass texture were underlined by medical endorsements, particularly for expectant mothers and the iron deficient. It actually has no more iron than any other beer.

GUM (CHEWING)

Not as popular as in the States, chewing gum in the UK is advertised mainly for its ability to clean your teeth after a meal. This has made it 'healthy' and socially acceptable, where once it was seen as bad etiquette to chew in public. Normal disposal seems to be the pavement, which explains the dark round marks found on the paving slabs of most cities.

✿ H ✿

HAGGIS

A Scottish delicacy, traditionally the heart, liver, and other offal of a sheep or calf, minced with suet and oatmeal and then boiled in the sheep or calf's stomach. Amazingly, for such a carnivorous dish, a vegetarian version is now commercially produced with the animal innards replaced with vegetables, pulses, and nuts.

HALAL

Meat that has been slaughtered and prepared as prescribed by Islamic law is increasingly easy to find. In 2006 the UK market for Halal grew by 300 per cent, though after a 2009 trial in one of its Southall restaurants, McDonalds took the decision not to introduce a special menu.

HANDSHAKES

Shaking hands was once the custom to prove you weren't armed. Nowadays, this is less likely to be the reason for the greeting, but a degree of discomfort is still present for Brits, and men in particular.

Most Brits seem incapable of deciding whether a handshake should be substituted for a hug or a European-style kiss, comprising two – or is it three? – pecks to the cheek.

The result is often a hurried and embarrassed combination of all greetings: handshake-hug-kiss-handshake. Then nervous laughter from all.

HANSARD

Arguably the world's dullest publication. Naturally, any comprehensive account of the announcements and daily business of a parliamentary debating chamber is going to be a little on the dry side. However, the modern Hansard actively rejects the idea of any possible entertainment for the reader, by failing to record the jeers, catcalls, and insults so characteristic of exchanges in the House of Commons. It also removes mistakes, tics, and inconsistencies from the speaker.

This does at least mean that a single edition of Hansard can be carried in a briefcase, rather than a suite of suitcases.

HIGHLAND DANCE

A traditional Scottish dance dating back to the thirteenth century, with some stylistic similarities to ballet. Although few ballet dancers are required to perform over a pair of unsheathed swords.

While graceful in appearance, training for the dance is gruelling – a typical six-step Highland Fling requires 192 vertical jumps. Tantamount, in terms of physical effort, to running a mile.

Predominantly a male event, the gender monopoly was broken spectacularly by Jenny Douglas at the end of the nineteenth century. Now ninety-five per cent of Highland dancers are female.

HIGHLAND GAMES

The good news for anyone looking to visit the Highland Games is that the name is generic, so competitions take place all over Scotland, and indeed across the world, throughout the year.

Supposedly owing its origins to attempts by the English to suppress military training in Scotland, the Highland Games feature a number of events that look remarkably similar to things you'd see in the Olympics, albeit with vastly heavier props.

The largest of the Games is held at the Cowal Highland Gathering in Dunoon, although the Braemar Gathering often gets the most media coverage, due to regular attendance by the Royal Family.

Even the least athletic of amateurs can take part in smaller Game events, with some cabers (long wooden poles) weighing a mere 100lb – in comparison to the 100kg beasts the best in the sport frequently compete with.

HOGMANAY

New Year's celebrations are important across the UK, but the Scots take particular pleasure in the period. Some say this is because of the importance placed on the shortest day of the year by the once-conquering Viking culture, or possibly because Christmas celebrations were viewed disapprovingly after the Protestant Reformation in 1560.

Welcoming 'first-footing' visitors at midnight bearing gifts of whiskey, dark fruit-cake, coal, or even salt remains an important tradition, especially when the guests forego the more traditional gifts of salt and coal in favour of the more practical ones.

HONOURABLE MEMBER

Referring to each other in the third person as 'The Honourable Member for (enter name of constituency here)' is supposed to take the sting out of debates in the House of Commons, but it hasn't prevented some memorable exchanges.

In the past Members have referred to each other as everything from 'a dead sheep' (Dennis Healey on Geoffrey Howe in 1978) to 'a sex starved boa constrictor' (Tony Banks on Margaret Thatcher in 1997).

In the wake of the expenses scandal of 2009, MPs unsurprisingly resisted calls for them to drop the 'Honourable', leading many to cite that it was such an attitude to self-governance that got them into trouble in the first place.

We leave you with Tony Banks again, who in 1994 described Terry Dicks as 'living proof that a pig's bladder on the end of a stick can be elected to parliament'.

HOODIES

Outside of Cistercian monasteries – which are pretty thin on the ground since Henry VIII dissolved them in 1530 – hooded clothing has recently become synonymous with living a life of indolence or illegality. This has little to do with the hood itself.

The reputation that comes with a hood has made them popular with consumers of all ages, looking to boost their street credentials. And the practical benefits are obvious to anyone who spends time in the open air for reasons other than dealing drugs, from triathletes to trainspotters.

Conversely, hoodies don't even need to be wearing hoods to be labelled as such. The tag is the latest in a long line of disparaging British labels attributed to anyone you'd rather not bump into on a street at night. Regional variations for wearers of such forebidding clothing include Jakie (Scottish) and Maggot (Irish).

HORSES

Once the main engine of transportation, the British now ride horses for pleasure, for work, for sport, to hunt with, and to race, as well as gambling on them. They even keep them as pets, but they never, ever eat them.

Or not knowingly, at least. A 2003 Foods Standards Agency investigation revealed that horse-meat could be found in many chorizo, salami, and pastrami products for sale in the UK, despite not being listed among the ingredients.

HOT-WATER BOTTLE

Extremely hard to find in Eastern Europe, the British home comfort of a rubber container with a plastic water-tight screw-top, filled with piping hot water, is loved the nation over. It's a less common possession now than it once was – possibly thanks to George Mikes' remark in 1946 that hot-water bottles are what the English had in place of a sex life.

In 2010, Holiday Inn announced it would be trialling the use of 'human' hot water bottles – staff members in hygienic all-in-one suits – in three of its hotels. Which, frankly, is just plain *weird*, no matter how hygienically they're suited.

HOVERCRAFT

Theorised in Sweden in the eighteenth century, tested in the 1930s by the Soviets, but generally regarded to have been invented by English-born Christopher Cockerill in the 1950s, the Air Cushion Vehicle is one of Britain's quirkier inventions.

Supported by a cushion of air, and propelled by fans, it can travel on sea or ground. Since 2000, it's no longer possible to take a Hovercraft to France, but you can still take one to the Isle of Wight.

'How are you?'

Bump into someone you know on the streets of Britain, and doubtless a comment as to each other's current state of health will be the first thing on both your lips, followed by a moment's consideration of the weather:

'How are you,' he or she will say.

'I'm fine, thanks,' you'll say. 'How are you.'

'Oh fine, fine. Gosh, it's cold.'

'Yes, it is cold,' you'll dutifully acknowledge.

'Well, must dash, lovely to see you,' one of you will say.

'You too! Let's grab a coffee soon,' the other will reply.

'Absolutely, let's.'

Notice that 'How are you' is not a question, even when said with an upwards inflection, so do not, under any circumstances, reply truthfully.

If the question is truly meant it might well be repeated, with a firm look and serious expression. At which point you would think it's possible to start divulging the terrible issues of your life.

Though if your friend then suddenly tenses up and breaks eye-contact, remembering they're 'late for something', you'll probably wish you hadn't.

Humour

British humour generally comes in one of six forms:

Sarcasm, where offence is intended, and the opposite of what is said, is meant: 'Oh splendid!'

Irony is more subtle, and less direct than sarcasm: 'Well, at least it's not raining ...' (just as the heavens open).

Wit is rooted in irony, but based on more astute observation; Oscar Wilde is generally regarded as the master: 'Always forgive your enemies; nothing annoys them so much.'

Satire is a mixture of all three. More good-natured than sarcasm, less subtle than irony, but very witty; at its best in *Private Eye* magazine.

Smut, which is everywhere. A sort of coy, non-explicit chortle, in a generally sexual direction.

Toilet, which is uniquely British, and nothing to be proud of.

HUNTING (FOXES)

Illegal in Scotland since 2002, in England and Wales since 2004, but still legal in Northern Ireland. The divisiveness bred by fox-hunting begins with how many would classify it – as a sport. For many of its supporters it is first and foremost an essential and valuable service; for its detractors, hunting remains a bastion of the class divide, not to mention cruel.

The delight of abolitionists as the bill made its passage through parliament was evident – but the passing also revealed a surprisingly vast number of supporters. Many who joined Countryside Alliance marches admitted ambivalence towards hunting, objecting to the imposition of laws by a metropolitan society on rural communities it had little understanding of.

The lack of natural predators for the fox has meant that there are estimated to be around a quarter of a million in the UK, fourteen per cent in urban locations. All of whom seem pretty nonchalant while rummaging through your bins, tending to stop only to glare back at you.

HYPERBOLE

In all but a few things, Brits are prone to understatement, if anything. They'll tend to blush rather than brag, and sidle rather than swagger. They'll exaggerate their circumstances (whether it be property or money, or how good they are at their job) – but in a very modest way.

Then there's sport, and sex. On neither topic must you believe a word Brits say, whether it's the difficulty of the catch, the world-class

nature of their performance, the size of their equipment, or the number of times they scored.

☙ ❄ **I** ❄ ❧

IMPERIAL WEIGHTS AND MEASURES

If resistance to a new decimal currency system was brief, a determination to hang onto the imperial pounds, ounces, and especially pints, has been dogged.

By law, traders' scales must display weights both imperially and metrically. As a result, large swathes of British life are governed by a system of measurements which everyone sort-of knows, but which few can convert.

As far as distances go, the conversion is simple for anyone who remembers the ruler they had at school, which was 12 inches/1 foot = 30cm (although it's actually 30.48cm).

Anyway, since there are 5,280 feet in a mile, and we've established that 1 foot is 0.3 metres (or 0.3048 metres to be precise), we can simply take the figure of 5,280 and … actually, maybe this will work better with weights …

So, to start again with an everyday item everyone's familiar with, a standard bag of sugar is 1 kilogram. Which is equal to 2.2046 pounds in the imperial system, where there are 14 pounds in a stone. So to convert …

Actually, once you accept that there are certain areas of UK life where each system holds sway, it's really quite simple:

> If you're buying or selling meat, fruit, or veg, you'll do it in imperial.
>
> If you're competing in any athletic event other than the marathon, you'll be measured by the metric system.

And if you're going to the pub, you'll need both, depending on whether you're drinking beer or wine.

So, good luck with all that.

INVASION

In the last two hundred years there have been two major credible plans to invade the UK, and on both occasions the distractions of other potential conquests (and Britain's island status) have prevented the seemingly inevitable.

Napoleon's late eighteenth-century plans for domination centred on taking control of the English Channel. His innovative approach was to attempt this aerially, through the use of hot air balloons. The plan was abandoned, due to unfavourable prevailing winds.

Hitler's Operation Sea Lion of 1940 had an invasion scheduled for September. He was equally struck by the possibilities of an air attack, but despite outnumbering them by 4:1, the Luftwaffe were unable to subjugate the RAF's aircraft. The Battle of Britain represented the first significant failure of the German War Machine – which swiftly turned its attention to the Russian front, and Operation Barbarossa.

All of which means that Britain hasn't been successfully invaded and conquered since the Norman Conquest in 1066, which many would say goes a long way to explaining much of the British character. Though only a brave few would go so far as to suggest the country could do with a good invasion to shake things up a bit.

INVENTIONS

The British are an inventive lot and can lay claim to bringing a number of useful items to everyday life. Here are thirteen of them:

Invention	Inventor	Year
Cat's eyes	Percy Shaw	1933
Crossword puzzles	Arthur Wynne	1913
Electric motor	Michael Faraday	1831
Flush toilet	Sir John Harington	1596

Gas mask	John Tyndall	1871
Internal combustion engine	Samuel Brown	1823
Penny-farthing (early bicycle)	James Starley	1871
Rubber band	Stephen Perry	1845
Sewing machine	Thomas Saint	1790
Toilet paper	Scott Paper Company	1879
Vacuum cleaner	Hubert Cecil Booth	1901
Viagra	Nicholas Terrett	1991
World Wide Web	Tim Berners Lee	1990

ISLE OF MAN

To the east of Northern Ireland, the west of England, the north of Wales and the south of Scotland sits the Isle of Man. With its own language (Manx) now revived in schools, and its own parliament (acts of British parliament do not apply to the island), the Isle has a feeling of being relatively isolated from mainland life. It is generally regarded as a tax haven: it has lower income tax than the mainland, and does not have any capital gains, wealth, or inheritance tax.

~ ❄ J ❄ ~

'JOBSWORTH'

The British have made a name for themselves as being lovers of rules and regulations. In 2009, Stewart Smith was delighted to be stopped by a Strathclyde Police Officer and handed a £10 note he had just dropped. An arthritis sufferer, Stewart quickly lost his smile when the same officer issued him with a £50 fixed penalty. For littering.

'JUST'

A word used by Brits to soften bad news, to disguise criticism, or in an attempt to pull a fast one. Deployed most commonly by those who like to think of themselves as direct, straightforward, and up-front, the word is usually teamed with hypothetical or rhetorical questions, an apologetic tone, and soothing adjectives, as in:

'I just wondered if it would be OK to grab a quick word with you, just very briefly?'

On hearing this you should prepare for the very worst.

✿ **K** ✿

KARAOKE

Japan's karaoke craze began insinuating its way into UK pubs and bars in the mid-1990s, but the ratings success of TV talent shows has kept this most seemingly un-British of pursuits incredibly popular. Between 2002 and 2008 the number of songs sung grew by an estimated fifty-two per cent, and the number of karaoke bars in London leapt from fifteen to fifty.

Sadly, the British prefer to be caught wailing distinctly un-British music, with only one Brit act making it into the top five for 2009's favourite karaoke choices – Queen's 'Bohemian Rhapsody'.

Though the patriotic among us could draw some comfort from the fact that Abba made it to the top spot with a song titled after the famous British victory at Waterloo.

KEBABS

The origins of this dish span the histories of the Arabic and Persian worlds, and its popularity across the world has led to the evolution of an incredible range of varieties, dependent on regional tastes and available ingredients.

All of which tends to be lost on the average Brit, who will be making a choice after a few seconds staring bleakly at an overhead menu after a heavy night's drinking. The 'choice' will be determined by how willing he or she is to wait for a tailor-made shish rather than just take the instantly available lamb or chicken doner.

A 2009 survey by local council body LACORS found that health-conscious Brits would be wise to endure the wait for the grilled shish option – doners were found to pack up to 1000 calories. Only thirty-four per cent contained just lamb, with some 'halal doners' even containing traces of pork.

KENDAL MINT CAKE

First formulated in 1869 by Joseph Wiper, and made in the Cumbrian town it takes its name from, this is even less of a 'cake' than the Jaffa Cake (which is technically a biscuit).

The name led New York customs officials to refuse entry for a consignment in the 1950s on the grounds that without flour, the combination of sugar, water, and peppermint could not be labelled 'cake'.

Its greatest claim to fame is a starring role in the rations of Edmund Hillary during the first successful ascent of Everest in 1953, where Sherpa Tenzing Norgay is said to have left some at the top as an offering to the gods.

Whether or not the story that Wiper's original creation was actually an accident (a batch of glacier mints made to the wrong consistency) is true, it's a recipe that's been developing ever since. The body of the cake is now made in three different varieties – white, brown, and chocolate coated – with a wide variety of flavours, from Rum & Butter to Winter Candy.

KETCHUP (HEINZ TOMATO)

Launched in the deep south of the USA in 1876 as a convenient alternative to home-made *catsup* (from the Malay *kichap*, which was originally a fish sauce, until US seamen began to add tomatoes). Heinz now sells 120 million bottles of this a year in the UK.

KNIGHTHOODS

The British honours system has been recognising 'merit, gallantry and service to the monarch' for over 650 years. Currently honours are bestowed according to a list of around 1300 names, published twice a year, on the Queen's official birthday (mid-June) and New Year.

A knighthood comes in one of four forms – Knight Grand Cross or Dame Grand Cross (both GBE) are more senior awards than Knight Commander (KBE) or Dame Commander (DBE).

Knighthoods are unique in giving the title of 'Sir' or 'Dame' before the name of the individual honoured, though the opportunity to engage in this form of social one-upmanship has been famously declined by physicist Stephen Hawking, composer Benjamin Britten, actor Albert Finney, and musician/actor/icon David Bowie, among others.

KRANKIES (THE)

British variety entertainment has thrown up some oddball acts over the years, but none come any weirder than The Krankies. The act itself is fairly conventional – a straight man's attempts at some bargain-basement magic are continually undermined by his chaotic companion, in this case a freckled schoolboy.

What makes the duo unique is the fact that they are actually a married couple, with the mischievous pre-teen Jimmy played by straight-man Ian's spouse, Janette. In 2003 Jimmy was voted 'Most Scottish Person in the World' by readers of the *Glasgow Herald*.

 **L**

LABOUR PARTY

Born of the Trade Union movement and Socialist political philosophy at the end of the nineteenth century, Labour secured its first parliamentary seats in 1900, winning two of the fifteen seats it contested on a total campaigning budget of £33.

It became the second largest party in the House of Commons in 1922, and formed the government's official opposition – a function that both political rivals and sympathetic admirers have often referred to as its 'natural' role. In power, its most enduring achievement was the creation of the National Health Service in 1948, a victory achieved in the face of opposition not only from the Conservative Party, but large sections of the medical profession.

Opposition was the position in which Labour spent around four-fifths of the twentieth century, with many accepting the then Shadow Chancellor Denis Healey's assertion that the party's mission was to 'erode by inches the conditions that produce avoidable misery'.

A recognition that some elements of its ideological make-up were never likely to be vote-winners increased as the party grew older and wiser. Pacifism was abandoned in the 1930s, Unilateral Nuclear Disarmament in the 1980s, and Clause 4 (which stated the party's commitment to nationalisation) in 1995, at which point Labour remarketed themselves as 'New'.

After the historic three back-to-back victories the party enjoyed after 1997, Labour introduced the minimum wage and successfully devolved power to Wales, Scotland, and Northern Ireland. It also went to war twice despite heavy public opposition, and suspended two elements of UK law that are key to civil liberties, 'double jeopardy' and 'habeas corpus'. With much of the electorate unhappy after years of political spin-doctoring, and Gordon Brown unable to secure a majority in the 2010 elections, the 'New Labour' label has already become a distant memory.

LAND

In 2009, the educational website Land Investment UK revealed that sixty-nine per cent of the land in the UK is owned by five separate landowners, the Dukes of Buccleuch, Northumberland, and Westminster among them. This might explain the size of the average British flat.

LEFT (DRIVE ON THE)

Evidence suggests that Brits have been keeping to the left since the Romans built their roads. Favouring right-handers, this allowed passing travellers the opportunity to wave, shake hands, or swing a sword with their preferred hand, as the situation demanded.

The UK shares this distinction with seventy-five other countries in the world, many of which have strong ties to the former Empire – though a decision to start driving on the right has proved a popular way to demonstrate independence from the colonial days.

The USA did just this, and is one of 163 countries and territories – forming a total of seventy-two per cent of the world's traffic – where the idea of driving on the left is seen as eccentric, if not downright perverse.

LIBERAL DEMOCRATS

The Lib Dems' biggest hurdle for the last few generations has been that the dominance of the House of Commons by representatives of Britain's two biggest parties is unlikely to be broken without a shift towards a system of proportional representation (which would favour neither of them).

As a result, Britain's third largest party was viewed as an 'also-ran' by the media and the electorate, and an irrelevance in the devolved parliaments where they were usually beaten into fourth place by Plaid Cymru or the Scottish National Party.

Despite this – and perhaps because voters have yet to experience the effects of their policies at national level – they are regarded sympathetically, and have promoted some notable characters to their highest ranks since being founded in 1988, including former commando Paddy Ashdown and Charles Kennedy, a charismatic 'Parliamentarian of the Year' who led the opposition to the war in Iraq. Nick Clegg (party leader since 2007) came out of nowhere in the 2010 televised debates and gained much needed media attention, even provoking some to say he might 'pull an Obama'. With neither Labour nor the Tories gaining a majority, the Lib Dems became the key holders to Number 10. Choosing to form a coalition with the Conservative Party, they've found themselves in a position of power for the first time in over 80 years.

'LITERALLY'

Used for emphasis, ninety-eight per cent of the time incorrectly:

'I was literally hanging by my fingernails'
'It literally cost me millions'
'I literally could have died of embarrassment'

LOCH NESS

Supposedly the home of Nessie, the vaguely glimpsed but never caught Loch Ness Monster. The freshwater lake in the Scottish Highlands is 40 kilometres long, 2.4 wide, and has depths of up to 230 metres, which is a very good reason why Nessie has continued to escape its hunters since the first 'sighting' in 1933.

LONDON

'When you are tired of London, you are tired of life' said Samuel Johnson, and while London is increasingly the place people come to work, rather than live, it's fair to say all life is there.

More than 300 languages are spoken by over eight million residents, it is home to twenty per cent of Europe's largest companies and the most expensive houses on the planet, and in 2009 was found to have the highest rate of income poverty in England.

It's certainly an expensive city, and getting from one side of its sprawling 610 square miles to the other can feel akin to travelling between different cities – even on the days when the ailing underground network system is working fine. But a trip to the Big Smoke (a name that's stuck from its nineteenth-century industrial smog-filled past) doesn't have to cost the earth.

Many of its greatest attractions, from the National Gallery to the British Museum are free to enter, as are all of its royal parks, as well as the not-so-royal ones. The Sunday morning flower market on Columbia Road, the markets around Brick Lane in the east and Portobello Road in the west, and the bookseller stalls on the South Bank, all provide respite from the rat-race of central Oxford Street.

≈ ※ **M** ※ ≈

M1–M90

The opening of the Preston by-pass in 1958 marked the start of Britain's turbulent relationship with its major (M) roads. Initially treated with the reverence afforded anything worthy of the space age, Britain's motorways have suffered from their own popularity, with the UK's thirty-two million vehicles making them the most congested in Europe in 2007.

The experimental speed limit of 70mph introduced in 1965 is rigorously monitored, and surveillance cameras across the network mean that anyone illegally present, from hitch-hikers to moped riders, isn't likely to be there for long.

While high-speed accidents still occur, motorways are relatively safe – of the 28,572 people killed or seriously injured on UK roads in 2008, less than four per cent had their accidents on a motorway. Add to that an absence of traffic lights and a relative lack of toll roads, and a motorway road-trip is usually a pleasant experience – if you can avoid the traffic.

It's worth knowing that though every motorway has a number, not all numbers are used – there's an M90, but don't go looking for the M88, as there isn't one. However, there is more than one of certain numbers – Northern Ireland has an M1, which offers better views and is generally a lot less congested than the English version.

With a characteristic concern for 'doing the right thing', signs along the English M1 warning that 'Tiredness can Kill' were removed in 1997 to prevent images of them appearing in photos taken of the hearse of Diana, Princess of Wales.

MAGNOLIA

The standard off-white/vanilla paint for the main living rooms in British houses, chosen for its neutral (read: bland) and therefore supposedly generally appealing colour. Since 1978. Or thereabouts.

MAGPIES

We are a much more superstitious nation than we like to admit, and most Brits on seeing a lone magpie will immediately look around for a second one.

If they can't find one, some will either salute the solitary bird (to show respect), or say out loud 'Good morning/afternoon, Captain', 'Hello Mr Magpie', or 'How is your/where is your wife?'.

This slightly bizarre behaviour comes from an age-old belief that magpies predict the future. There is an accompanying rhyme that tells what sort of future you can expect:

> One for sorrow, Two for joy,
> Three for a girl, Four for a boy,
> Five for silver, Six for gold,
> Seven for a secret, never to be told,
> Eight for a wish, Nine for a kiss,
> Ten for a bird that's best to miss.

In Ireland, the alternative 'Five for a wedding' is often used.
We are an odd bunch.

MANAGEMENT

Management isn't what it used to be in the UK, or at least the title of 'manager' certainly isn't. Attempts by corporations to make their poorly paid workers feel better about their lot have led to an over-proliferation of the title at the bottom end of the hierarchy.

It's common now for a retail outlet with two members of staff to have two managers – one store manager, and one assistant or deputy manager. The title is also handed out where those in seniority are hoping to protect themselves from actual interaction with the general public. So a request to see or speak to the manager will grant you an audience only with the person who's there to deal with you, rather than anyone in a position of real power.

Recently, many organisations and individuals avoid the title due to its divisive nature, and opt for something more inclusive and 'fun', such as Team/Section Leader.

MANCHESTER (MANCS)

A phoenix from the ashes, Manchester is a changed city. After an IRA bombing in 1996 destroyed many buildings in the centre, the tearing down of the more dangerous council estates at the turn of the century, and the arrival of the Commonwealth Games in 2002 (and the associated building of new sports facilities necessary for such an event) the centre is rejuvenated.

With a lively gay district near the canals and now occupying a central location in the country, Mancs is generally thought of as a rougher, cooler alternative to England's capital.

The city was not only mother of the mid-1990s 'Madchester' scene that provided Britain with a welter of new music like Oasis and the Chemical Brothers, but also of the Hacienda, a club that proudly kick-started much of Britain's early-1990s rave scene.

MAPS

Britain's Ordnance Survey Maps have been providing hikers, geographers, and the scout and guide movement with beautifully detailed, cryptically coded paper representations of the landscape since 1791.

Understanding the various legends and keys – being able to read the map, in other words – is much like getting into jazz: at first it'll seem bewildering, then frustrating, then it'll all click into place. Or you'll get lost and end up in a crap pub eating stale crisps and listening to Abba.

MARATHONS

Despite being a younger event than the New York race that inspired it, and until 2005 featuring a cobblestone stretch even the thought of which has participants breaking out into a cold sweat, the London Marathon is regularly voted the best race of its kind in the world.

Since 1981, the circuitous route via some of London's greatest buildings (including St Paul's, Buckingham Palace, and St James's Palace) does its best to distract entrants from the pain, and the race's party atmosphere and an early spring climate seem to have finally found a genuinely appreciative audience. The annual April event has become a great day to be in London – as long as you aren't planning on driving anywhere.

Close on its heels in terms of number of participants is the Great North Run in Newcastle, a half-marathon which started in the same year as London's race.

In Northern Ireland, both the Newry City and the Mourne Way marathons in County Down have spectacular views of the old city and coastline respectively. In Wales, the Anglesey Marathon promises beautiful and serene surroundings, while the nearby Snowdonia Marathon offers gruelling conditions and unpredictable weather. The Moray and Loch Ness marathons in Scotland give runners and spectators the prospect of a dolphin or (if you're lucky) a Nessie sighting.

MARMITE

The British equivalent to Australia's Vegemite, the brown, yeast-based spread. Now infamous for its parent company's main advertising campaign, which proudly boasts that many people hate the taste. The number one food missed by British ex-pats, its name is said to derive from a French soup, *petite marmite*.

'MATE'

The default term of endearment exchanged between men in informal settings across the British Isles. Used across broad strata of social situations, from first introductions to familiar greetings, the only time it can work against the user is when the atmosphere is tending towards

the hostile. Any wannabe mediator suggesting 'Calm down, mate' is likely to be told 'You're not my mate, mate!'

MENSA

The perception that Britain is a land of dry, slightly snobbish, academically gifted but socially inept library-dwellers is not without reason. Thinking along similar lines, a British doctor and an Australian barrister established a society whose only criterion for entry was a demonstrably massive intellect.

This is proven by taking a supervised IQ test, though you'd think if you were clever enough, being supervised wouldn't necessarily stop you cheating. Formed in the UK in 1946, the title Mensa doesn't actually stand for anything. It's derived from the Latin for 'mind' and 'table' – as you'd already know, if you were smart enough to be a member.

The idea has been successful enough to spawn fifty affiliate organisations around the world, the largest of which is in the US, with nearly 60,000 members (almost double the number of eggheads as the UK chapter).

Despite understandable differences in the way groups are run, members of all nationalities sign up to the same mission statement – to use their massive combined intellect to benefit humanity. It appears the best way to achieve this philanthropic gesture is by completing crossword puzzles and lateral-thinking visual games.

More recently the Mensa board-game has been providing brain-training fun for all the family.

MI5/MI6

In other words, Military Intelligence, departmental sections 5 & 6.

MI5 is the Security Service (the UK's security intelligence agency), and is responsible for 'protecting the UK, its citizens and interests, at home and overseas against major threats to national security'.

MI6 is the Secret Intelligence Service (and the working home of Ian Fleming's fictional spy James Bond), responsible for 'gathering intelligence outside the UK, in support of the government's security, defence, foreign and economic policies'.

Rather than 'spies', they refer to their staff as 'agents', but only when an employee works as part of the Covert Human Intelligence Sources.

Under the Security Service Act of 1989 the Service is apolitical, so both sections supposedly operate independently of the government. That said, the Home Secretary is accountable in parliament for MI5, and the Foreign Secretary for MI6.

For those wondering what happened to the first four MI sections, they used to cover code-breaking, Russia, Europe, and aerial reconnaissance, respectively, but were either discontinued, or absorbed into The War Office, MI5 and MI6, and Government Communications Headquarters (GCHQ).

MI5's motto is 'Regnum Defende' (Defend the Realm). MI6's motto is 'Semper Occultus' (Always Secret).

MID-LIFE CRISIS

A familiar, and not particularly Brit-centric notion, where people panic that they have lost their youth, and set about trying to reclaim it. Americans might buy a Porsche, get plastic surgery, and sleep with someone they shouldn't. Brits might get an allotment, try a dieting milkshake, and join a book club.

MILKMAN

An almost extinct species, these rare breeds were most prevalent in the twentieth century. Often announcing their early-morning arrival with a shrill whistle and the buzz of the electric motor powering their movement (the milk-float), they have been almost wiped out in all but the most suburban and remote parts of the UK. Sadly, competitive supermarket prices and a move to the metric system has made the

delivery of freshly bottled pints of milk, cream, or orange juice all but a fading memory of an Olde Britain. For the record, the colour-coded aluminium tops of the pint bottles (which were often then collected for charity or school art classes) were:

silver – whole milk
red striped – semi-skimmed
blue hatched – skimmed
gold – Jersey milk
green – unpasteurised

MILLENNIUM DOME

A flagship project which was designed to simultaneously regenerate an economically depressed region of east London and provide Britain with a great new public building to mark The Dawn of a New Millennium!

In reality, the Dome was pretty much a failure on every criterion it could be measured by, though it does remain the largest construction of its kind in the world. Which is nice.

Based on the history of its construction, the white elephant that hoovered up so much of late 1990s arts funding looks likely to remain a large pachyderm for some time. Delivered behind schedule and over budget, the exhibition that marked its opening was slated by the media, and audience numbers never came close to matching those projected.

In November 2000, the failed heist of the Millennium Star, a diamond held on exhibit with a value of over 200 million pounds, brought more drama to the building than it had previously witnessed, but sadly didn't turn into a regular show with hourly performances.

The exhibition closed after one year, at which point the question of what anyone would want with a giant dome was finally raised. With almost depressing predictability, the Dome then lay largely unused for several months, at great public expense.

It nearly became a giant casino, before being bought at a bargain basement price by a private concern that has since made a huge commercial success of it as a music and sports venue – the O2 Arena – at which Prince has played, Michael Jackson nearly played, and on which Bon Jovi played a roof gig in 2010.

MILTON KEYNES

A commuter-city, 72km north of London. One of the UK's 'new towns', it was designed in the late 1960s to be a city of the future, with plenty of pedestrian subways, a grid-system of wide roads, and an edict that states 'no building can be taller than the tallest tree'.

The reality is somewhat different. The road system is confusing, the pedestrian subways are impossible to navigate, and the tree edict was quietly scrapped: the Milton Keynes Shopping Centre is alarming in its size – with over 166,000 square metres of retail floor, it has a number of trees *inside it*. (By comparison, the vast Westfield Shopping Centre built in central London in 2008 has a mere 150,000 square metres of floor space).

As a result, the city has become known as a not especially pleasant place to visit, and is frequently the butt of jokes.

MINI

An iconic British car, renowned for its low fuel consumption, idiosyn-cratic style, and easy parking – though it isn't particularly recommended for anyone over 5ft 6in.

The original version started out as Austin Drawing Office project number 15, and was made world famous by its use in the 1969 Michael Caine film *The Italian Job*.

That version of the car is a lot harder to spot now as manufacture was halted in 2000. The revamped Mini began production in Oxford in 2001, and has been tremendously successful (with a million sold in six years).

The newer model is both much more comfortable than the original, and a product of the BMW corporation. Which makes it about as British as a sauerkraut sandwich.

Monarchy (the)

There is a view that the Windsors are little more than a first family, rather than a royal one. The ongoing soap opera of the younger members of the Queen's family, in a society that has become media obsessed has only reinforced this viewpoint. Which is a shame, as it obscures a lot of the valuable work done by the monarchy.

The boundaries that determine attitudes to the monarchy within Britain are more generational than they are national. Older generations are more likely to share a broad enthusiasm for the institution and its individual personalities than the younger, who can't see the point of such a transparently absurd and outdated means of governance, even if it is now ostensibly only symbolic.

Despite this, members of the dynasty have been able to define themselves with an individual voice, and if you are drawn into a conversation on the Royal Family there are some subjects that are (relatively) safe to talk about:

- the excellent work of *The Prince's Trust*, heir-to-the-throne Prince Charles' youth charity which helps train disadvantaged young people, and offers start-up grants to businesses;
- likewise, the *Duke of Edinburgh Awards*. Aimed at 14–25-year-olds, the youngsters must set and achieve an objective in four areas – volunteering, physical, skills, and expedition. The awards are Bronze, Silver, and Gold, but to gain the highest award, a fifth area, residential, must be achieved, by staying and working away from home for one week;
- the world-class equestrian abilities of Zara Phillips, eldest granddaughter to the Queen and twelfth in line to the throne;
- the two young Princes William and Harry, children of Charles and the late Princess Diana, who (despite their nightclub forays and paparazzi-bashing) have shown an admirable commitment to their work within the armed forces, at a time when the services have been stretched to breaking point both by their many overseas commitments and by funding cuts back home.

MOORS

Tracts of open, rolling, unused land, covered with heather and patches of marsh, are rather characteristic of Britain. Despite the undoubted beauty of much of Britain's moorland (as with any wilderness) there are both inherent dangers in terms of remoteness and associations that aren't entirely positive.

The Yorkshire Moors exert a strong draw on anyone who's read Bronte's *Wuthering Heights*, largely for their blustery and untamed representation in the book. On a sunny afternoon, though, you'd be hard pushed to find a better picnic location.

Dartmoor in Devon is the largest open space in southern England and devastatingly beautiful, despite the fact that it also provides the surroundings for the high granite walls of HMP Dartmoor, one of the most imposing prisons in the country.

Unsurprisingly, like any urban area of wasteland, moorlands throughout the UK have also been the sites of the very worst kinds of criminal activity. The so-called 'Moors murders' took place in the Saddleworth Moor (Greater Manchester) in the 1960s. The perpetrators, Ian Brady and Myra Hindley, are two of the most reviled criminals in recent memory, having abducted, assaulted, killed, and buried five children on the moors. One of their victims' remains is yet to be found, although a new search was begun in 2010 by the Ogwen Valley Mountain Rescue charity.

MORRIS DANCING

A traditional English dance, which until very recently was men-only, involving stomping and hopping around, while holding handkerchiefs, clapping sticks together, and (optional) bell-wearing.

Utter, utter madness, but a brilliant example of the unbridled silliness Brits can get up to, and oddly enough (considering the dancing, the bells, the waving of sticks, and the handkerchiefs) one of the few occasions a Brit won't feel self-conscious.

Moustaches

A facial feature once rarely seen without a beard attached, the moustache used to be the sign of a true gentleman, but is now considered more an indication of eccentricity.

The fact that many politicians are now thought to be unelectable until they part ways with their moustaches gives you an idea of how much things have changed.

The Handlebar Club in London has been running since 1947, and its only requirement for membership is 'a hirsute appendage of the upper lip, and with graspable extremities'. It takes its name from the flattened 'w' type moustache (which looks a little bit like the handlebar of a bicycle).

Mr/Mrs/Miss/Ms/Master

With men, it's easy. They're all *Mister*. No one has been referred to as *Master* since knickerbockers went out of fashion for men. With the female of the species, chances are you'll just get it wrong.

Miss can imply belittlement, while *Mrs* seems to suggest advanced age, and in both cases there's a subtextual question present: whether the lady in question is married or not. Unfortunately, *Miss* implies she has every reason not to be, and *Mrs* implies that purely based on appearance, she probably ought to have settled down by now. The scheme hatched to circumvent all of these potential pitfalls was the term *Ms*, pronounced as if you have an angry bee trapped in your mouth.

The simplicity of *Ms* is that it bypasses this patriarchal system of address, which for centuries has defined women by their marital status (while recognising men in their own right).

However, address some women as *Ms*, and they may insist on being referred to as *Mrs*, possibly as a way of announcing their own lack of strident feminist beliefs.

As we say, chances are you'll just get it wrong.

~ ❋ N ❋ ~

'NAFF'

For a brief window in the 1980s, this was the word to use if you were referring to something 'uncool'. Using it nowadays, however, will mark you out as being distinctly so yourself.

'NANNY STATE'

The phrase has been around at least since the 1960s, and implies a government that protects rather than one that governs. A survey run by the King's Fund (an independent think tank) in 2004 found that many of the people asked would favour a state where the government controls diet and public smoking.

From banning conkers in school (due to Health and Safety issues), to fining people for feeding ducks in a park in late 2009 (it was considered littering), some say that with all the signs telling you where to go, what to do, and how to do it, the UK is already en route to a Neo-Puritanism.

It probably won't be long before we aren't allowed to say such things.

NATIONAL PARKS

Britain's National Parks were legally brought into being in 1949 with the National Parks and Access to the Countryside Act. Until that point, entering these areas of natural beauty was illegal, and you could be prosecuted for trespassing.

Indeed, the Kinder Scout Mass Trespass in 1932 (named after the highest point in the Peak District), and another later that year in Castleton, brought over 10,000 walkers out in protest.

Now 'Britain's Breathing Spaces' are free for all to wander through. Over thirty-six per cent of Britain's land area is now protected under the Act, with fifteen national parks (ten in England, three in Wales, two in Scotland) in all.

1951 – Peak District, Lake District, Snowdonia, and Dartmoor

1952 – Pembrokeshire Coast and North York Moors

1954 – Yorkshire Dales and Exmoor

1956 – Northumberland

1957 – Brecon Beacons

1989 – The Norfolk Broads given equivalent status to a National Park

2002 – Loch Lomond and The Trossachs

2003 – Cairngorms

2005 – New Forest

2010 – South Downs

NATIONAL TRUST

The National Trust is a body devoted to protecting buildings, bridges, and beauty in all their natural forms. Founded in 1895, it owns in excess of 3650 historic houses, gardens, and monuments, all of which are open to the public (at a cost).

Many of its attractions draw huge crowds on Bank Holidays and throughout (what passes for) summer in the UK. After luring steady numbers of new members for many years, the NT has rapidly become one of the best loved of Britain's institutions.

Just don't expect much change from a fiver for a cup of tea ...

NEIGHBOURS

For reasons clear to absolutely no one, the British seem to do all they can to avoid their neighbours.

While this can be convenient (particularly for politicians looking to claim expenses on properties they don't actually live in), should you actually need to speak to them in the event of their wisteria interfering with the growth of your hibiscus, then you might be somewhat stuck.

Writing a letter to your next-door neighbours falls just on the wrong side of formality for most British residents, unless next door is a mile or more away. This means your only option is to lurk by your front door, waiting to pounce as they enter or leave their own abode, curtains twitching.

The alternative is to cross your fingers and hope for a sunny day, giving you a chance to chew the fat over the back garden fence, like they do in TV adverts.

NEIGHBOURS (SOAP OPERA)

Looking for things to fill the schedules in the late 1980s, the powers that be at the BBC happened across an Australian soap opera that was attractive for two reasons. It was available at (a) a very reasonable price, and (b) in such quantity it would allow them to write off a whole two and a half hours per week, bridging the difficult slot between Children's BBC and *The Six O'Clock News*.

This cunning plan to capture as large an audience as possible by filling as much screen time as possible with smiley attractive young people (where possible idly wandering around in their swimwear) worked rather well.

Not only did it work, those responsible for bringing the show to our shores also had an unintended hand in shaping the makeup of the music chart for years afterwards. Australian soap stars repeatedly found themselves in the top ten of the charts in the late 1980s and early 1990s.

A generation later, *Neighbours* is still with us, albeit in a less prominent place in the TV schedules, with memories of Scott and Charlene, Harold's 'drowning' and amnesia-ridden return, and Bouncer the dog not quite fading fast enough. Fortunately, the music scene has shaken off all soapy contenders – aside from the dance-disco-queen Kylie Minogue.

Newspapers

Newspapers in Britain fall roughly into two categories: tabloid and broadsheet, named after the way the newspapers are printed: tabloids in portrait; broadsheets in a wider portrait and then folded in half, making them look landscape.

Both styles have varying levels of quality and political motivations. The tabloids (or redtops, due to their distinctive red-banner title) are the source of gossip, semi-naked women, and very little of what could generally be considered 'news'.

In recent times, some of the more journalistically credible broadsheets have started printing their newspapers in the tabloid format, trying to make their papers more compact and easy to read.

Here's a list of the main national newspapers, and their target market, with Rupert Murdoch's news corporation *News International* running *The Times* (and *The Sunday Times*), the *Sun* and the *News of the World* until its closure during the 2011 phone-hacking scandal:

The Financial Times (FT): printed on distinctive salmon-coloured paper, for the city/financial sector.

The Times: the classic image of a British gentleman clad in bowler hat, suit, and umbrella, also has a copy of *The Times* under his arm. Anyone delivering more than a couple of copies of the massive *Sunday Times* has their work cut out.

The Independent: as the name suggests, the Indy aims to be politically unaligned, but is actually fairly liberal, and is a strong voice for environmental issues.

The Guardian: generally regarded as the most liberal, at least in terms of the viewed readership, thought to be the artists and artisans of Britain. Only slightly unfairly nicknamed the *Grauniad*, due to a period of frequent typos. On Sundays printed as the *Observer*.

The Telegraph: traditionally seen as the most right-wing paper.

The Daily Mail: the most alarmist paper, in its depiction of threats to the nostalgic idea of the 'British way of life'.

The *Sun/Mirror/Star/News of the World*: the red-tops. If it's loud, outrageous, unobjective, biased, based on hearsay, without general regard for the feelings of those they write about, and documented with pictures taken by the paparazzi, it's likely to be printed here. The *Mirror* is the most left-wing, the *Sun* is the most popular in the UK in terms of sales (and also the home of the Page 3 girl), and the *Star* can barely be classified as a 'news' paper. Prior to its demise, the *News of the World* was known for breaking gossip-related scandal first.

9/11

The shockwaves of the destruction of the twin towers were felt all over the world. Of the 329 non-US foreign nationals killed, sixty-seven were UK citizens. As news of the tragedy broke across the UK, airports and stations at major cities were closed down, leaving many with no way of getting home.

Large parts of Britain were suddenly eerily peaceful and the skies were empty, though many pubs, bars, and restaurants found themselves doing an unusually brisk and sombre trade for a Tuesday night.

The official response was notable for its quite uncharacteristic sensitivity and sincerity from Prime Minister Tony Blair. Always more comfortable with broad sentiment than factual detail, he captured the nation's mood both in the sentiments he expressed and the way he expressed them.

The decision by the Royal Household for the Household Cavalry to play the American National Anthem on 12 september at Buckingham Palace showed their improved grasp of the value of deviating from routine, in reflection of significant events; a choice clearly appreciated by those Americans grieving in the UK.

Nobility (forms of address to)

Styles of address abound in a monarchy like the UK, and are therefore a potential minefield for anyone concerned.

Entire books are written on how not to confuse an Earl with a Viscount, or how to avoid mistakenly proffering a 'Your Holiness' instead of an 'Excellency'. The good news is that paying attention to such absurd, arcane, and usually unearned honours is deeply unfashionable. Should you happen upon the wrong title form, chances are it will be more embarrassing for the Lord, Duke, or Baron to point out your error.

Still, if you're moving in lofty circles it might be worth brushing up on the correct way to refer to the different ranks of nobility, of which there are a multitude. Though thankfully not quite as many as in Germany.

Here's a brief list of the most important:

King/Queen	Your Majesty
Prince/Princess	Your Royal Highness
Duke/Duchess	Your Grace
Earl/Viscount/Baron	My Lord/Your Lordship
Countess/Viscountess/Baroness	My Lady/Your Ladyship

North/South divide

A major divide in Britain has often been seen between a cultured, metropolitan, civilised south and a supposedly unrefined, industrial, barbaric north, with the schism occurring at the Watford Gap (that stretch of the M1 approximately eighty miles north of London's Charing Cross).

The roots of this apparent division are undeniable: the concentration of political power in Westminster and the setting of the UK's two leading academic centres in southern England, against the importance of manufacturing, mining, and engineering in the industrial centres of Sheffield, Liverpool, and Newcastle. And the manual, constructive work of the north contrasts heavily with the high-end retail, banking, and creative endeavours that tend to be associated with the south.

While the North/South divide is now fading, it is one that many seem to want to keep alive and kicking. Former Labour Deputy Prime Minister John Prescott continues to gain mileage for his 'northern working class' credentials, as if these somehow transform the middle-class activities of, say, cheating on your wife with your secretary and applying mock Tudor beams to the front of your house (and charging the taxpayer for it) into part of an ongoing North/South class war.

If a divide exists now at all, it tends to occur more along the fault lines of rural/urban, or even simply between London and the rest of the UK.

'NOTHING'

In the UK, 'nothing' is very nearly always 'something':

- The unhappy expression on the face of a friend will always have been caused by 'Nothing', should you choose to ask 'What's wrong?'
- The husband caught in front of a mirror wearing a dress and high heels who is asked 'What are you doing?', will invariably, pale-facedly reply, 'Nothing.'

In both instances, 'nothing' is the response of someone who doesn't want to burden others with his or her own personal troubles, but would probably appreciate the follow-up question, 'Are you sure?'

At which point, burdening can commence.

NSPCC

Formed in an 1880s London where you couldn't walk five paces without tripping over the slumped figure of a dusty, malnourished six-year-old orphan chimney sweep, snatching a half-hour's sleep before starting the next eighteen-hour shift.

The tremendous National Society for the Prevention of Cruelty to Children seeks to 'eliminate the abuse, mistreatment and neglect of minors'. It certainly says something about the latent British attitude of the time towards children: the only legislation in nineteenth-century Britain that allowed for any form of child protection was championed by the RSPCA, and invoked on the grounds that a child was a 'small animal'.

The organisation's remit is broad and far reaching; it has the power to apply for 'care and supervision' orders, and its effective merger with the confidential helpline *Childline* in 2006 has consolidated its position as one of the UK's most high-profile and respected charities.

Nursery rhymes

Many of the best-loved nursery rhymes contain archaic language that is baffling to adults, let alone the children they recite the nonsense to.

By way of an explanation, many parents will have told their questioning infants that 'curds and whey' is a popular dish in the UK, or that everyone in Britain relaxes in front of the TV on their favourite tuffet, with their pockets stuffed full with posies.

Well, we don't. And we're not sure what any of those things are either.

 O

Oak

The oak tree is a classic British image that has popped up on more coats of arms than any other tree, and has long been a symbol of solidity, tradition, and service to a higher order. The oak has featured on the back of the pound coin, and an oak leaf is the emblem of the National Trust.

It has its roots firmly in mythology, being sacred to the druids and the Anglo-Saxons, and the gateway between worlds for the Celts. It provided shelter for King Charles II from the Roundheads in 1651 (the eponymous Royal Oak in Boscobel Wood) and the timber for Francis Drake's and Horatio Nelson's adventuring ships, and was heralded in Rudyard Kipling's poem 'A Tree Song'.

On a darker note, its sturdy trunk and strong branches once made it a favourite with hangmen looking for an impromptu gallows.

OCCUPATION

The British fear of direct, open questions means that it can be quite difficult to discover what people do for a living, unless they offer the information up themselves.

Because Britain has blazed a trail for bizarre and inexplicable job titles and descriptions, even if you get an answer, the title might not shed that much light on what it is they actually do.

With this in mind, respond to all questions about your job by saying you're 'in business'. Either that, or plump for the easy-to-picture teacher, police officer, or doctor, and hope that no one in your vicinity is suddenly taken ill, needs arresting, or teaching a lesson.

OFFAL

For a country of people quite particular about their food, there has been a surprising resurgence in nose-to-tail dining (so-called because nothing between nose and tail goes to waste). While faggots, the offal-meatballs that were once a traditional dish in the English Midlands, have become less popular, dedicated offal restaurants offering roast bone marrow, suckling pigs, or pigeon and trotter pie have been springing up all around the UK.

Although some may baulk at eating hoof, cheek, intestine, heart, or head, the snack of a crispy pig's ear or the light-bite of kidneys on toast can grab the attention of even the least courageous diner.

OFFICIAL RESIDENCES (ROYAL)

The Queen has five official royal residences: Buckingham Palace in London, Windsor Castle, Sandringham House in Norfolk, and the Palace of Holyroodhouse and Balmoral Castle, both in Scotland.

Balmoral and Sandringham are private residences, while Buckingham, Windsor, and Holyroodhouse have sections open to visitors. The Union Jack flag is flown above whichever the Queen is

currently residing in, the medieval equivalent of a neon light flashing 'The Queen is IN'.

OLYMPICS

For reasons best understood by the International Olympics Committee, the summer games have only ever been hosted by one UK city, which will happen for the third time in 2012.

In terms of spectacle and organisation, the next London Olympics will inevitably draw unfavourable comparison with the

Beijing 2008 games. But it's worth noting that whatever happens, 2012 will be a very different affair to the last two London Olympics.

In 1908, London inherited the games from Italy (which had an eruption of Mount Vesuvius to deal with) and had rather short notice (less than a year) to organise the event and build the stadium.

The bicycle polo and tug-of-war both thankfully went off without a hitch, but the murky swimming pool (also the venue for an international fly fishing event) led to complaints about a lack of lane markings.

Forty years later, saddled with massive war debts to the USA (the final payments of which were made in 2006) and with the end of rationing still six years away, the 1948 London Olympics were known as the 'Austerity Games'.

The main athletics stadium was actually a converted dog track and car headlights stood in for floodlights. But at least towels were provided for competitors after their cold showers (for a small hire charge).

This make-do-and-mend attitude may have made the games a humble affair, but it also made the event unquestionably representative of what it was to be British back then. Whether the same attitude holds up with the next games remains to be seen.

'ORWELLIAN'

Eric Blair was one of the great British writers of the twentieth century. He's more familiarly known by his pen-name George Orwell, a name that has moved into common parlance to refer to any overly watchful or freedom-crushing entity.

The widespread usage is utterly unaffected by the fact that his dystopian masterpiece *1984*, which features such an entity, goes unread by large numbers of his countrymen (who nonetheless claim to be fans of it).

The now omni-present CCTV camera, and the mining of personal information by any organisation (governmental or otherwise) that cares to, have led many commentators to suggest that British society is increasingly Orwellian. With some justification.

Owain Glyndwr

The last Welshman to be honoured with the title of Prince of Wales, Owain matched many of the achievements of the Scottish braveheart William Wallace – with one notable exception.

Glyndwr led an ultimately unsuccessful but valiant uprising against English rule in the opening years of the fifteenth century, and in so doing gained significant victories in combat against overwhelming odds, most notably at Mynydd Hyddgenn in 1401.

However, while Wallace was brought to trial and inevitable execution in England, the Welshman not only evaded capture but seemingly disappeared altogether, leading to much speculation as to how he spent his retirement.

Less internationally known than Wallace – mainly because no one has made a Hollywood movie about him yet – he is nonetheless an important figure to his countrymen, and a significant character in Shakespeare's rollicking history *Henry IV Part One*.

'Oxbridge'

While a village bearing the name Oxbridge can be found in the county of Dorset, the name is more commonly used as a conflation of Oxford and Cambridge – the cities considered to be the top two centres of learning in Britain.

As such, they enjoy a healthy rivalry, not only in terms of academic prestige but also in sporting prowess, most obviously displayed by their annual Boat Race on the River Thames.

Admission to either institution is highly prized, and the term is often used when referring to students seeking places at either or both: 'applying for Oxbridge'. Given the competition for places, traditionally such a student would most likely be very bright, very rich, or very both. In recent years the universities have (while maintaining the highest levels of academic ability) made efforts to shrug off such elitist impressions, and ensure that their student bodies are comprised of a wider social mix.

Both maintain they are the oldest, having been founded in the early thirteenth century; until the nineteenth century they were the only universities in England.

'Oz'

Not a fantasy world a long way from Kansas, but Australia, a country which shares much with Great Britain – a language (usually), a queen (controversially), and an obsession with cricket (undeniably).

As with any relationship between two entities that share a lot of DNA, abiding affection demonstrates itself mainly through bickering, a calm sharing of ideas, and a lot of distance.

∿ ❋ **P** ❋ ∿

PARKING

There are parts of the UK – the A7 running out of Edinburgh, the B5105 in north Wales near Ruthin, Northern Ireland's Antrim coast road, or the toll section of the M6 – where driving is truly blissful. But wherever you are and wherever you're going in the UK, rest assured that parking will be a total nightmare when you get there.

'Decriminalised parking enforcement' – the civil enforcement of parking regulations carried out by civil enforcement officers (the handing out of tickets by parking wardens, to you and me) – has led to at least three times as many penalty charges being issued to errant drivers.

Introduced in London in 1994 (and enthusiastically adopted everywhere else soon after) these charges have become important revenue streams for the local authorities enforcing them. Predictably, then, the staff they employ are performance-managed and incentivised to issue as many tickets as possible.

From red lines, yellow hieroglyphics, and residents-only bays, to no-waiting zones manned by CCTV cameras, there are now more ways for you to incur a fine than ever. If in doubt, assume you are parked illegally, and expect a fine of £50 or more to be winging its way to you soon.

And bear in mind that as far as a CCTV camera is concerned, if you've come to a complete stop at the side of the road, you've parked.

PHONE BOX (RED)

First cast in concrete in 1921, and ever since set in stone as an indicator that a movie is set in the UK, at its height the red phone boxes numbered over 70,000.

Privatisation of British Telecom in 1984 led to a replacement of the old boxes with a modern, darkly tinted box, later equipped with internet and email capability.

Once the main social hang-out for teenagers with nowhere else to go, the arrival of the ubiquitous mobile phone has meant fewer people need such boxes of communication. Still, following awareness that Giles Gilbert Scott's familiar design had become a British institution, a number of the red boxes have been listed, protecting them from future development plans.

Others have been turned into temporary libraries, used in art installations, or sold off. Some, like their sister-icon the double-decker bus, have had shower cubicles installed.

PLAIN ENGLISH CAMPAIGN

An independent body that has been campaigning for the use of straightforward, easily understood language (particularly in politics) since 1979. And which, with the best will in the world, seems to be fighting a losing battle.

POET LAUREATE

Unsurprisingly, some of the most famous poems written in the English language have come from the British Isles. Geoffrey Chaucer,

Robert Burns, Cecil Day-Lewis, and Dylan Thomas all made their names in the form.

So if you're looking to turn professional poet, there are probably far worse lands to ply your trade, as for centuries the reigning monarch has chosen a poet to produce works on a range of subjects of national importance. The Poet Laureate has been engaged by institutions as diverse as a Category B Men's Prison, the *Guardian* newspaper, and Tottenham Hotspur Football Club.

Chaucer was referred to as Poet Laureate (or rather *versificator regis*) and Shakespeare's contemporary Ben Jonson was James I's poet-in-residence. Neither William Wordsworth nor Nicholas Rowe held the post for very long, both dying relatively quickly after being appointed.

Queen Elizabeth II has seen five poets hold the post during the course of her reign: Cecil Day-Lewis, John Betjeman, Ted Hughes (after Philip Larkin refused), Andrew Motion, and in 2009, Carol Ann Duffy, the first woman to be made Poet Laureate.

POLITICAL CORRECTNESS (PC)

Words, beliefs, and attitudes that have passed so far out of fashion that they have become unacceptable for public airing are termed 'politically incorrect'. '"Unacceptable" according to whom?', is a good question.

If any public figure lets slip something even mildly inappropriate (i.e. racist, sexist, or any other *ist*), the chances are the *Daily Mail* newspaper will kick up a fuss until the rest of the media hangs, draws, and quarters all those who have forgotten to fully prepare any off-hand comments they intend to make.

To say that something is 'politically correct', therefore, usually carries the implication that whether or not something is true, it would be inappropriate to say otherwise.

Oddly enough, the phrase would never be applied in relation to social practices that were once fully accepted (if distasteful) facts of life, but which are now universally reviled, such as slavery or domestic violence.

The expression has also come into use to describe anyone seen to be highly aware of the (largely unwritten) dictates on what is socially acceptable to say: they will be referred to as being 'very PC'.

Ironically, this is not generally considered to be a compliment.

PONTEFRACT CAKE

Named after the Yorkshire town of its origin, it is actually a small liquorice sweet, and not a cake. The use of the word *cake* comes from its original meaning, of 'a shaped and compressed mass of food', as in a *cake of soap*.

POST OFFICE

A post office has become an increasingly difficult thing to find in Britain's towns and villages. Two thousand five hundred sub-post offices have been closed since 2007.

For many Brits, the post office is far less important for posting items than it is as an informal community centre for paying bills, collecting state pensions, and completing application forms.

That said, using the Royal Mail still remains the most economical way of sending letters and parcels to your loved ones. Despite a general perception that both standards and morale within the Royal Mail are steadily declining, the service it offers is one that most users rate very highly.

It is a service particularly appreciated by the members of parliament who supported the sub-post office cull, but were foresighted enough to ensure that this wouldn't impact their own lives too much. Three post office counters are situated within a five minute walk of the Houses of Parliament.

PRIVACY

Nothing divides British behaviour quite like the attitude to privacy. The default setting is one of polite respect for the privacy of others, and a tendency to keep oneself to oneself.

This attitude is conveyed by a tendency to withhold information on the most seemingly innocent of subjects, unless directly questioned on them. That reticence is backed up by a set of physical behavioural patterns, designed to minimise exposure and occupy as little space as possible (folding arms, looking down, pretending to use a mobile phone), all signals that will hopefully be interpreted as 'Do Not Disturb ... Please!'

All this changes, of course, with even the most moderate exposure to any form of alcohol. At which stage any and every subject is open to discussion, with gestures and expressions becoming wilder and wilder. The normal British desire for bags of personal space goes out of the window, and volume levels go up to eleven.

PROMS (THE)

The BBC Proms is an annual classical music festival, which has been held at the Royal Albert Hall in London since the 1940s. There's a mistaken air of elitism around The Proms which is in direct contrast to its intended remit.

The Proms began in 1895, wishing to 'present the widest range of music, performed to the highest standards, to large audiences'. It was the brainchild of Robert Newman, who wanted classical music to reach a wider audience than normal. He hit on the idea of offering more popular music, lower prices, and – most importantly – a promenade setting, whereby much of the audience stands rather than sits.

The seventy Proms concerts play from mid-July to mid-September, there is no dress code, all are broadcast live, and to get a ticket to the famous and fabulous Last Night of the Proms, you have to have booked for at least five other concerts. 'Prommers' are well known to sleep outside the Hall to secure their favourite standing spot inside. You can also apply to join a ballot to gain pairs of the last remaining tickets for the final night.

Public/Free House

A quintessentially British institution, and a home-from-home for many. Pubs in Britain have been brought to their knees over the course of the 2008–09 recession, with over 2300 pubs closing. The government's pub minister (who'd have thought it) has been fighting to keep many more open, by offering the public the chance to invest in and/or buy the pubs.

Pubs are either owned by a brewery (Public House) or by the landlord (Free House). Expect a wider variety of beers at a Free House, and a selection of the brewery's own at a Public House.

'Pulling'

Or, 'negotiating a successful encounter with a prospective sexual partner'.

This charming phrase can mean anything from acquiring a phone number to actually bedding, but can only be achieved once with any given individual.

Its association tends to be with the more casual end of the relationship market, and anyone looking to engage in such behaviour is said to be 'on the pull'. It is, though, a term that can be used by married couples, in reference to the time they first got together – 'Remember the night I pulled you?'

Classy.

Punctuality

British people tend to have an absurdly precise approach to punctuality. That's not to say they won't be late for things, but if they are, then they will have a good reason for it – a train running late, a car breaking down, or an Act of God.

If a Brit is late to meet you, he or she will unreservedly and repeatedly apologise, and you shouldn't refer to the slip again. If you're late to meet a Brit, no amount of apologising will make up for your tardiness, and you will be repeatedly reminded of your rudeness.

PUNK

The late 1970s/early 1980s music and life movement that will not die, and thank goodness. Often thought of as coming from the working classes, a lot of the Punk movement actually came from a middle-class anger and frustration with the state and society.

The effect on modern music never seems to diminish. Many artists (rightly) associate the style with a terrific energy and freedom of expression. True Punk has nothing to do with drugs or alcohol, but frequently has a political agenda. The other, more familiar side of Punk music – getting trashed, taking drugs, and so on – has unfortunately taken over the image of this music scene and is not, technically, Punk.

While younger people's lifestyle choices of long, colourfully spiked hair and piercings have been replaced by the black, tight-fitting clothes and eye shadow of the goths/emos, Punk is here to stay.

~ ❋ **Q** ❋ ~

'QUAINT'

A word that will instantly mark you out as a tourist, should you use it. While many features of the British Isles may indeed seem *rustic*, *picturesque*, or *whimsical* (and so thereby, *quaint*), to describe them as such to a Brit will almost certainly cause offence.

There is an assumption that by 'quaint' you mean that something is old-fashioned or odd, and that you're being patronising. The British will only ever use the word *quaint* ironically about things that are either outdated, or there solely for the benefit of tourists.

QUASI-AUTONOMOUS NON-GOVERNMENTAL ORGANISATIONS

QUANGOs were introduced to the UK in the 1980s as part of a pledge by the UK government to reduce the size of central government, thereby devolving power.

After Gordon Brown became prime minister, annual spending on QUANGOs rose twenty-five per cent, from £37 billion to £46.5 billion, funding organisations from Job Centre Plus to The British Potato Council, as well as local NHS trusts.

Considering very few people could actually name a QUANGO, or indeed, explain what one is, it could probably do with being a slightly less opaque scheme.

QUEEN (THE)

While the British retain a great deal of affection for their monarch Queen Elizabeth II, there is now a general consensus that her role in the life of the nation recedes annually in terms of actual importance.

She (or rather a representation of her) had great support in 2006, when a film was made detailing the Royal Family's reaction – or apparent lack thereof – to Princess Diana's death in 1997. *The Queen* enjoyed considerable success both commercially and artistically: it made over £850,000 in its UK opening weekend, over $122 million worldwide as of May 2007, and gained both an Oscar and two BAFTAs.

The ruling monarch has made an annual speech, *The Royal Christmas Message*, every year since 1932. The *Queen's Speech* (as it is popularly, if mistakenly, labelled) is broadcast via radio and television twice on 25 December, after which it is never repeated.

'QUEER'

A mainstay of the language of P.G. Wodehouse's character Bertie Wooster and Enid Blyton's Famous Five series, meaning 'strange', it was appropriated to refer to the gay/lesbian/transgender community in the last years of the twentieth century.

It is now part of the vast arsenal of put-downs available to anyone commenting on anything or anyone not subscribing to a heterosexual lifestyle, though thankfully it seems to be receding from use.

Like *gay* (which used to just mean 'happy') most English speakers tend to stay away from it altogether for fear of causing confusion, and substitute it with the far less ambiguous 'odd'.

QUESTIONS

British conversation is marked by the predominant use of closed questions – that is, questions which can be answered only with a 'Yes' or 'No'.

So, rather than asking an open question such as 'What did you think of the concert?' a British person is more likely to ask 'Did you *enjoy* the concert?' which is technically a closed and leading question.

Although the use of closed questions encourages one-word answers, to respond with one would, bizarrely, be considered ill-mannered. Indeed, the slight lead given by a closed, leading question allows the respondent to push the conversation in whichever direction they like, thus:

'Did you enjoy the concert?'

'Yes, very much. Although I would have liked it more if they'd played some of their older material.'

'Absolutely! And it *was* all over quite quickly!'

Once the positive starting point of 'we both enjoyed the concert' has been agreed, it's then possible to move on to the favourite British conversational pastime – listing the faults – though this is still done under the auspices that the event witnessed was essentially 'good'.

A warning to visitors to these lands: the majority of British people would prefer it if you didn't question their national institutions (the monarchy, the game of cricket, and the weather). Our own derogatory comments about these things may seem to be an open invitation for you to join in, but this is most definitely not the case.

QUEUES

Queuing is such a solid part of British culture it has become almost mythical in status, and a cliché to mention it. But it's easy to underestimate just how very seriously we take the business of queuing. It really can be a matter of life and death.

It was reported in January 2009 that one reason why more British people died during the Titanic disaster was because the Brits queued for the lifeboats, whereas others did not.

Clearly, the Brits have a longstanding respect for queue protocol, but jumping a queue will rarely get you into actual trouble. Generally, the result will be a sales-person simply refusing to serve you.

In a very extreme case, you may hear the odd 'tut', or possibly a muttered 'There is a queue, you know'.

'QUICK DRINK'

In the USA, an invitation to 'drinks after work' is rarely the bacchanalian celebration of the working day's end it sets itself up to be. Particularly on either coast of the States, 'drinks' will actually be singular rather than plural, and frequently not even alcoholic in nature.

Conversely, in the UK you're more likely to find yourself invited for 'a drink' (note the singular use) or its ubiquitous and typically British apologetic sibling, 'a quick drink'.

You should not be taken in by either. Whatever form it's issued in, the invitation to go for 'a quick drink' will very rarely ever mean 'one'. Or, for that matter, be 'quick'.

'QUITE'

Qualification is at the heart of the British mentality. In many cases it will actually negate the adjective that follows it, so if you hear someone say 'Yes, I thought that it was quite good…' then it's likely he or she thought 'it' wasn't good at all.

As with most things British, the underlying desire to promote harmony is undermined by the use of tiny linguistic markers, a function also served by the words 'just' and 'actually'.

Particularly different from American usage, where *quite* means 'very', and is strongly positive.

❧ ❁ **R** ❁ ❧

Rabbits

Originally brought over from France in the twelfth century and adopted by the Royal Family (which kept them to hunt), the rabbit is the third most popular small mammal to be kept in Britain as a pet.

This may be down to its cute floppy ears, twitchy little nose, and darling little tail. Or it could be that a combination of its legendary breeding ability, and its suitability for a featured role in a good stew, has made it a cheap, easy, and potentially nutritious candidate for domestication.

Richard Adams' bestselling novel (and the subsequent heart-breaking film) *Watership Down* captured the particular plight of the rabbit in the UK. Like most of the rest of the animal kingdom, the story sees the little hop-hops forced to relocate to make way for new-build one-bedroom apartments that no one really wants to live in.

Rabbits can see behind themselves, but have a blind-spot directly in front of their faces. Much like a Brit.

Railways

British Rail remains a popular two-word excuse for the late arrival of countless Brits, but the company British Rail hasn't actually existed in any meaningful way since the mid-1990s, when the rail network was privatised. Its corporate symbol, reminiscent of a mangled swastika, however, can still be spotted outside the UK's stations.

If you're looking to blame someone for your train's late arrival, over-crowded carriages, or toilets that would be deemed shocking at music festivals, your options are to curse:

- *Railtrack*, responsible for maintaining the rail network, or
- one of the many franchises who operate the rolling stock you find yourself sat in (should you be so lucky as to actually find a seat).

RAIN >> WEATHER

RED ARROWS

Many Brits hold a fond memory from their youth of seeing the nine red Hawk jets criss-crossing the sky, trailing streams of red, white, and blue smoke.

The daredevil team of pilots still perform their outlandish manoeuvres, including their signature 'diamond nine' formation, where they fly ridiculously close together in a diamond shape:

A section of the Royal Air Force, the RAF Aerobatic Team have been flying and performing at air shows since 1965, and their first female pilot joined the team in 2009.

The organisers of the 2012 Olympics deemed the Red Arrows 'too British' to take part, a qualification that you'd hope will not affect our athletes intending to participate.

RELIANT ROBIN

A three-wheeled car (two at the back, one at the front), that was prevalent in the 1970s and 1980s. Iconic in its own meandering way, its production stopped in 1981, temporarily resumed in 2001, and was finally halted in 2002.

It famously graced TV screens for decades in the comedy series *Only Fools and Horses*, and was transformed into a space shuttle (which promptly exploded) for the car show *Top Gear*.

The vehicle's secondary function was to transport people or things from A to B; the primary function was as an object for drunk people to push over late at night.

REPERTORY THEATRE

A system of small-scale theatre production that was most prevalent during the 1940s–1960s. It's a tradition that stretches back to Shakespeare's time and beyond, whereby a company of actors (led by an actor-manager) rehearse play 1, then rehearse play 2 in the daytime while performing play 1 in the evenings, and so on, usually with four plays 'in rep(ertory)'.

Repertory theatre provided the backbone of Britain's smaller-scale and touring theatrical scenes, and the basis for many of today's leading British actors' training and initial employment. The cuts made by the Conservative Party in the late 1970s are generally held to be responsible for the demise of the centuries-old tradition.

REVOLUTION

There hasn't been a revolution in Britain since the deposing of Charles I in 1649. It's a slight linguistic sleight of hand, though, as we've had revolts, rebellions, civil wars, and been involved in both international and world wars.

Still, over 350 years without the deposing of the head of state is, in European terms, quite a long time. The last time the country was invaded was 1066, which is also none too shabby.

ROSES (WARS OF THE)

The Wars of the Roses were a thirty-year (1455–1485) family feud between the House of York and the House of Lancaster for the throne of England, so called because the emblem of both Houses is a rose.

In order to show which house you'd aligned yourself with, supporters of York wore a white rose, while supporters of Lancaster wore a red.

The 'wars' brought about the restoration of Edward IV on the English throne and the collapse of the Plantagenet dynasty, and are generally considered to signify the end of the medieval period and the beginning of the renaissance.

They also ensured that any sporting contest between teams or institutions from York and Lancaster would be for ever more similarly dubbed a 'War of the Roses' – usually with each team wearing the appropriate white or red colours.

Though when cricket is being played both teams tend to stick with white.

ROUNDABOUTS

Roundabouts are a common enough feature of British roads, and could in many ways be symbolic of the wider social, behavioural, and ceremonial aspects of life in the UK.

They are things which are successfully navigated by Brits so acquainted with the rules attached to their use that they barely give them a second thought. But for anyone visiting Britain they are arcane, impenetrable enigmas, more likely to engender vehicular paralysis and leave you feeling that roundabouts should be consigned to the dustbin of history.

Should you find yourself near the Hertfordshire town of Hemel Hempstead – and you'll have no good reason to – you might want to check out the town's 'magic roundabout', a large central roundabout surrounded by enough smaller satellites to confuse even the most experienced of drivers. Make sure your car insurance is fully comprehensive before planning a trip.

ROWING

As modes of water-based transportation go, rowing has to be about the most ungainly. It's extremely hard work that'll leave you with an aching back and calloused hands. Plus you'll be travelling backwards for the duration of the journey.

Perhaps, though, it's this combination of stoic suffering and the focus on what's been, rather than what's coming, which has ensured the ongoing popularity of rowing as both a British pastime and a competitive sport.

An Olympic sport since 1900 (the 1896 rowing event in Athens was cancelled due to bad weather), the UK currently ranks third on the medal table, after Germany and the USA.

The two big occasions in the rowing calendar are the Henley Royal Regatta, which spans five days over the first weekend in July; and the Boat Race, which (despite a seemingly democratic-sounding name) is only open to entrants from Oxford or Cambridge University. Like a variety of things in the UK.

ROYAL MARINES

The UK's marine corps, which specialises in amphibious, mountain, and Arctic warfare. Formed as part of the Naval Service in 1755, the commando force is trained to fight in any terrain.

Not surprisingly then, much of the thirty-two weeks' training takes place at night on Dartmoor. The initial commando training (before going on to specialist training) involves a final week-long test:

Saturday	Endurance course
Sunday	Rest
Monday	Nine-mile speed march
Tuesday	Tarzan assault course
Wednesday	Thirty miler
Thursday	Failed test re-runs
Friday	Failed test re-runs

As Commander-in-Chief of the British Armed Forces, Queen Elizabeth II is the overall head honcho.

RSPB

Despite having similar staffing levels to the RSPCA and enjoying a broad level of support from the UK population, The Royal Society for the Protection of Birds is often seen as something of a poor relation to its sister organisation. Founded in 1889, its remit tends to be broader

than the RSPCA, and tied into wider conservation issues. Subsequently, its 1500 employees and over 14,000 volunteers spend their time and resources maintaining over 150 reserves across the UK.

They also carefully monitor breed numbers and generally try to promote ornithology, both to the general public and among its community of bird-watchers, sweetly termed 'twitchers'.

With over a million members, it is the largest wildlife conservation charity in Europe.

RSPCA

In existence for a more than half a century before someone had the bright idea of setting up a similar organisation for human children (see NSPCC), the Royal Society for the Prevention of Cruelty to Animals has familial organisations in Scotland (SSPCA) and Northern Ireland (USPCA).

Its balance sheet reflects the devotion of the British to the welfare of animals – or at least to the animals they have a soft spot for and aren't planning on shooting, eating, or skinning for clothes any time soon.

Despite having no formal powers of entry, arrest, or investigation, it routinely undertakes private prosecutions against anyone considered to have neglected an animal's wellbeing, and employs nearly 1500 staff within a regimented and uniformed hierarchy.

RUGBY

The 'hooligan's sport played by gentlemen' remains more upmarket than football, both in the conduct of its players and the behaviour and background of its followers.

Scandals around violent play, simulated injury, and drug-taking may have had an impact on its clean image, but this has largely been countered by the firm handling of individual incidents by the sport's governing bodies.

One of the great appeals of the game is that it allows the Welsh, Scots, English, and Irish to compete on a relatively level playing field, and home nation games attract huge good-natured crowds in pubs all over the UK.

Anyone unfamiliar with the game will quickly recognise its similarities to both American and Australian Rules football, though it has less padding and less forward passing (i.e. none of either).

Visitors to the UK should not be drawn into discussions on the differences and relative merits of Rugby League and Rugby Union unless they have an eye for detail and plenty of time on their hands. Nor should they ask for an explanation of any of the rules, particularly the intricacies of the 'offside' ruling.

✢ ❃ S ❃ ✢

SAGA

A company that specialises in holidays and insurance for the over fifties. SAGA has bucked the trend for call-centres based abroad by outsourcing only as far as Kent, which is always going to do well with its UK customers.

Since commencing operations in 1984, the SAGA magazine has gained a readership of over 100,000 per month, and its company name has become synonymous with the increasingly affluent and influential 'grey' market.

Influenced by the term for someone who has drunk too much lager, the label applied to an older person behaving in a reckless or drunken manner on a SAGA holiday is 'Saga lout'.

SALOON BAR

Pubs in the UK were often divided into two – the Public bar and the Saloon bar – and you would be presented with two doors on entering such a premises. Divisions like these are less common now, but can still be found in older pubs that haven't been refurbished.

The saloon bar tends to be more refined, with comfortable chairs, tables, and perhaps a fire-place. The public bar houses the juke-box, pool or snooker tables, and fruit or games machines.

The atmosphere changes radically between the two: one is for quietly supping ale, and the other is definitely more for slamming tequila shots while attempting 'that' trick-shot with the cue behind your back.

SALVATION ARMY

Founded in East London in 1865, the 'Sally' Army has arguably lost the high-profile spot it once occupied in the UK's charitable sector, largely due to the direct nature of its religious affiliations.

Nonetheless, its work with some of the most vulnerable members of society both in the UK and worldwide means it retains huge support, and its appointment of female ministers within its organisation blazed a trail in eliminating gender discrimination from the Christian movement as a whole.

Although it has spread across the world, its HQ and training college are in London. Its brass bands (with donation boxes) are a regular sight on summery Sunday mornings, whether you want to hear them or not.

SAMARITANS (THE)

Started in 1953 by the vicar Chad Varah, when he noticed there was no emergency service that citizens could turn to when contemplating suicide.

Now covering the UK with over 200 branches, the Samaritans (originally known as Befriending, but then renamed after the biblical parable of the Good Samaritan) provide 'confidential, non-judgmental emotional support, 24 hours a day for people who are experiencing feelings of distress or despair'.

Run by volunteers, many of whom are there simply to listen, the Samaritans is a terrific organisation that has not only saved thousands of lives, but has provided troubled people in the UK with someone to turn to in times of need.

SANDWICHES

The fourth Earl of Sandwich probably didn't realise the consequences of his actions when he took a slice of something tasty and put it in between two pieces of bread.

Now a staple part of the British lunch, the sarnie/butty/barm-cake snack-meal existed long before the eighteenth-century aristocrat, but his name has been claimed for it, after others started ordering 'the same as Sandwich'.

SAS

The Special Air Service is a regiment of the British Army, commonly referred to as The Regiment. It's been involved in every major British conflict since World War II, and entry requires a six-month test of strength, endurance, and resolve.

Candidates must undergo a Basic Fitness Test, a Combat Test, and a series of cross-country marches (at the end of which there is an 'Endurance' test in which they must complete a forty-mile march in less than twenty hours, carrying a load in excess of fifty-five pounds including water, food, and rifle).

THEN comes the jungle phase (often in Malaysia or Brunei) where candidates learn weapon and tactical training using live ammunition. This is followed by survival, escape, and evasion training. Training ends with the grim-sounding thirty-six-hour Resistance to Interrogation test.

Successful candidates are then assigned to an Air, Boat, Mobility, or Mountain Troop, and undergo a twelve-month probation period, before being fully accepted into the SAS.

A former SAS soldier, 'Andy McNab' (his pen-name for a series of books about The Regiment), wrote the best-selling *Bravo Two Zero*. It detailed his time both active and captured in the Gulf War.

The motto of the SAS is Who Dares Wins. Rightly so.

'SASSENACH'

A word used by the Scots to refer to the English in a derogatory way. It literally means 'an English inhabitant of the British Isles', which is like referring to a rat as 'a rodent inhabitant of the house'; it doesn't go as far as calling that inhabitant a 'pest', or even 'vermin', but it gives the subtle notion that the rodent's presence in the house is unwelcome.

The word originally came from the Scots-Gaelic for 'Saxon', and has similar sounding Irish and Welsh variants ('Sasanach' and 'Seisnig', respectively).

However assuredly and politely they might insist otherwise, there's long been an underlying contempt for the English that doesn't look set to change any time soon. Exactly why this is the case is unclear, but it certainly doesn't have anything to do with the centuries of English rule under which the Welsh, Irish, and Scots were forced to suffer.

SAUNAS

Go to a sauna in Eastern Europe, and you'll most likely receive a solid supply of beneficial health treatments, and emerge pink and fresh.

Go to a building advertising 'Saunas' or 'Massage Parlour' in the UK, and you'll most likely receive a different kind of service, and probably emerge without your wallet.

Although it would be slanderous to suggest all saunas or massage parlours are houses of ill-repute serviced by ladies of the night, it would equally be foolish to expect only improved health from whatever lurks behind the red-neon-lit windows.

SCHOOL SYSTEM (THE)

The school system in the UK is somewhat complex, even for those who have been through it and come out the other side. There's a commonly held belief that the two main options are Public and Private, but that's not the case. The big divide here is actually between Public and Private on one hand, and State Schools on the other.

Public and Private schools are, potentially, open to all, but both types of establishment will charge a fee. This is often in the region of many thousands of pounds per term, though you may be able to gain a scholarship to cover this.

The main difference between Private and Public is that the latter are members of the Headmasters and Headmistresses Conference. The HMC is an association of the leading independent schools in the country, to which Private Schools cannot gain membership (though a limited number of particularly outstanding State Schools can join).

Because they are effectively operating outside the state sector, Public and Private schools will generally have greater freedom in determining their syllabus and/or entry requirements, although they will still have to comply with government legislation on both.

State Schools – of which Comprehensives are the most common – do not charge to receive students. Paid for by taxes, their syllabuses have to comply with all government rulings or they will risk the wrath of OFSTED, the schools' inspectoral body, which after visiting all the State Schools publishes a league table, based on how an institution has fared in various areas.

None of this information is taught in schools...

SCIENCE

In 2009 a report from the Department for Business, Innovation, and Skills stated that UK science is the most productive and efficient in the G8, accounting for just under eight per cent of the world's scientific papers. It also mentioned that more Nobel Prize winners have come from Cambridge University than from any other institution in the world.

While we've invented some pretty interesting things (see Inventions), we still haven't sussed out how to make tea pour from a pot without it dribbling. But we're working on it.

SENTIMENTAL

Most British people will say that they are not sentimental. But regardless of any claims made by individual Brits on a personal level, all the evidence suggests that, on a national level, Britain is one of the most sentimental places in the world.

Of course it can be hard to define at what point a genuine concern becomes a mawkish sentiment, but on a wide range of issues – which animals you should and shouldn't eat; the traditions (and particularly the ceremonial attire) attached to the workings of parliament; the institution of the monarchy; the system used for weights and measures; the design of currency – the default British attitude tends to be one of sentimental attachment to outdated or nonsensical dogma.

Which sort of accounts for Morris dancing.

SHAKESPEARE/'SHAKESPEARIAN'

One of those parts of British heritage that most people feel they ought to know more about and have read, but don't and haven't. Named man of the (last) millennium and the greatest writer of the English language, his name is now often attributed to anybody that speaks in a heightened, theatrical, or affected way.

The writer of thirty-nine surviving plays and some terrific poems over the course of a twenty-year career in Elizabethan London, Stratford-upon-Avon's most famous son – the 'immortal Bard' – has become one of Britain's most famous exports, and can lay claim to much of the incoming tourist trade.

Odd then, that a surprising number of Brits doubt William Shakespeare was the real author of the plays, claiming other, better-educated writers of his day (including Sir Francis Bacon, the Earl of Oxford, and even Queen Elizabeth herself) were responsible for these great works.

Such doubt in one common man's genius and talent probably says more about the Great British cynical attitude of 'If it looks too good to be true, then it probably is', than anything else.

SHEDS

A (normally wooden) structure at the bottom of the garden, where gardening tools, sun-loungers, old bikes, table-tennis bats, flower-pots, and pornography are kept.

SHETLANDS

The group of 100 or so islands that form the northernmost points of the UK. For anyone willing to make the trip they offer a great deal – phenomenal light, dramatic landscapes, and the chance to see the aurora borealis in winter, should the clouds hold off.

Pawned to Scotland in 1469 by a hard-up King Christian I of Denmark and Norway (who never got round to buying them back), the islands retain a culture that's unlike any other part of the UK.

Scandinavian influences have stayed prevalent in the cuisine, music, and especially the Up Helly Aa annual fire festival. There's a refreshing lack of tacky gift shops, too.

SLAVERY

The UK's record on slavery is a mixed one. On one hand, it made huge profits from the business at its height in the eighteenth century, and ports at Bristol, Liverpool, and London were major transit centres responsible for the industry's unfortunate cargo.

On the other hand, Britain's anti-slavery movement's vigorous campaigning led to its abolition in 1807, with emancipation for all by 1833. In order to support the ruling, the UK's naval fleet committed more than ten per cent of its manpower to help end the trade.

SMOKING

Since the EU law came into effect in July 2007, it is illegal to smoke in 'workplaces and public spaces' – basically anywhere where someone is forced to passively smoke your smoke, by virtue of the environment you're sharing. The Health Act of 2006 clarifies these spaces as 'offices, factories, shops, pubs, bars, restaurants, membership clubs, public transport and work vehicles that are used by more than one person'.

This has meant that in an effort not to lose too much business, nearly all pubs, clubs, and bars have tried to provide smoking areas directly outside. These range from luxurious sheltered and heated seating areas, to what seem to be animal pens – enclosures surrounded by metal railings.

The only indoor spaces in which it's still legal to smoke, are, interestingly:

asylums
hotels
nursing homes
offshore oil rigs
prisons
submarines
stage/television/film sets

Smoking cannabis in the UK is illegal, but the government keeps changing its mind on the penalty for, let's say (just to pick an example randomly out of the air) smoking cannabis in a park on a summer's day... It's also generally forbidden to light barbeques and let your dog treat the park as its own toilet. But people still do.

Snow

The flippant thing would be to say that there are two types of weather in Britain, wet rain and frozen rain, but that would be uncharitable, and not entirely accurate. Britain's seasons do tend to blend into each other, so it's not particularly out of the ordinary to have a warm, sunny day in January, a snow-storm in April, and heavy showers in July.

The difference is that when there's an excess of any type of weather, it always seems to take the British slightly by surprise. Society grinds to a halt when snowfall that wouldn't be noticed in other countries lands on these shores.

To be fair, such surprise isn't restricted to the white stuff: people get soaked when it rains, not having brought their umbrellas out with them; they get badly burnt in the sun, having neglected to buy sun-tan lotion; they get frozen, having decided to wear two pieces of silk and a piece of string on a night out in November.

Technically, it is only considered to have officially snowed on Christmas Day if a snowflake hits the roof of the Met Office, which gives you an idea of the generally high and specific expectations the British tend to have of their weather.

SPEEDBUMPS

Once rather charmingly referred to as 'sleeping policemen', speed-bumps have become a feature of pretty much any minor roads that were once a pleasure to drive down.

Originally focusing on residential areas that had become unofficial short cuts for bypassing more major routes, cars began to use other side-streets to avoid the new speed regulators. These other side-streets then received speedbumps, and so on.

Residential speedbumps were supposedly designed to bring a car's speed down to 20mph, though some are steep enough to consider breaking out the winch.

It is, perhaps, ironic that the UK has more speed cameras per head than any other country on earth. While their deployment has helped both to cut road traffic accidents and to free up policing manpower, they remain a source of major irritation for British motorists.

Most UK drivers seem to have the same attitude to both attempts to regulate speed – foot to the floor until the very last moment before coming into the range of bump or camera, drive nonchalantly until back out of range, then speed off to the next traffic jam.

SPELLING

The spelling of the English language is, most would agree, more than a little odd. This is less surprising when you take into account that it has developed over the course of one and a half millennia.

In its nascent years, it was heavily influenced by French and Latin (for example, the word 'debt' had its 'b' added to pay homage to Latin, once the language of the elite).

More and more rules were added until people tried to standardise spelling in the eighteenth century – by which time the language was already an unruly adolescent of 1300 years, throwing letters all over the place.

Add to that the daft US variations (color vs colour, humor vs humour, sidewalk vs pavement) and you get the surly, complicated adult language that will make even a native speaker stop to soundlessly mouth out '*i* before *e*, except after *c* ... except when ... um ...'

SPITTING

Spitting on the street in the UK is considered unseemly at best and aggressive and offensive at worst. Nose-picking is fine though, and when you're sat in a traffic jam on a Sunday, it's verging on mandatory.

STARING

Staring is not something particular to the British, but apologising for it is. Should you find yourself in company and staring blankly into space for more than a couple of seconds, you should apologise immediately, and briefly inform everyone what had been occupying your thoughts (or an acceptable substitute should that 'something' be better not shared).

This is particularly true if your stare has been brought on by the sight of something admirable, in which case you should immediately compliment the owner on whatever it was, and then start talking about the weather.

STRANGERS

The warning to 'never talk to strangers' is drilled into British children even before they are of an age to comprehend such a concept.

It's largely for this reason that the British are appalling at introducing themselves and each other, and renowned for wishing to avoid any kind of accidental physical contact.

Even the simple act of clearly stating your name and offering a hand to shake can have a remarkable impact. Given the generally observed rules on talking to strangers, the recipient of your approach will assume one of four things: that you are insane; that you want money; that you are already known to them; or all three put together.

As options one and two tend to come with clear visual signifiers (foaming at the mouth, ill-matched shoes, high visibility tabards bearing the name of a charity), most people will assume the third and happily proceed to ask you how your family is doing.

By the time it has become clear they don't actually know you, it will be too late for them to do anything about it without appearing rude. Ironically, there's a good chance you'll become the best of friends. Who don't know each other's names.

'STUPID'

The first marker in the lowest foothills of offensive language. Foolish words or people can be referred to as 'silly' without causing offence even to the most fiery of Brits:

'Oh you ARE silly!'

would normally be followed by much giggling.

However, describing someone's thoughts, actions or beliefs as 'stupid':

'Oh, don't be stupid!'

will, for some reason, cross over the line, igniting a Brit's pride, and possibly land you in fisticuffs territory.

SUNDAY TRAVEL

Don't. Just don't.

Britain's ailing railway system is in a state of constant repair and upgrade, as more and more lines strive to provide high-speed services around the country.

The upshot of this is that most of the repair work is done on the least busy day of the week – Sunday. The upshot of *this* is that going *anywhere* by train will probably involve getting off a train, and onto a bus – the infamous Rail Replacement Service – for at least part of

the journey. To avoid such complications, many will choose to drive instead, which means the roads are a nightmare too.

In 2009, a train journey from Kettering to London (81 miles, an hour by train, around two hours by car) became a 295-mile journey around the country, due to engineering works. The route suggested by the rail company took eighteen hours by train (the same route by car would take six hours), involving:

> seven changes
> five bus rides
> a trip on the London Underground
> and an overnight stay in Milton Keynes.

And while most of that is relatively manageable, no one wants to spend the night in Milton Keynes.

The train company later simply advised not to even bother trying to travel on a Sunday, which is a little like a pub advising you not to drink alcohol because you'll get drunk.

And really, *really* don't try to travel by train on a Bank Holiday weekend. Stay where you are and find a newspaper and a good Sunday Roast instead.

SUPERIORITY

Most British people do not necessarily consider themselves automatically superior to every other being on the planet.

That said, the stand-offishness exhibited by many, particularly when they're meeting people for the first time or are in unfamiliar surroundings, can often be mistaken for just that.

At the height of its influence, the British Empire was the most expansive the world had known. The legacy of that realm is a people whose collective behaviour resembles that of retired prime ministers: they know they've had their time at the centre of power, and will do their utmost to be polite about whoever has taken their place, but they don't have to like it.

Ironically, the only British people you're likely to encounter who are immediately approachable, genial, and seem genuinely comfortable in their own skins, are those privileged enough to have received the best education that money can buy.

The flipside of this is that these people will consider themselves automatically superior to every other being on the planet.

SWEARING

Despite an apparently overwhelming array of ways to cause offence to the British, there are now really only a small number of words in the English language that are still considered really insulting.

The severity of all of these will, of course, depend on the delivery, but many newspapers have begun printing these words in full and without asterisks:

'shit' now heard regularly on the street, and the mildest of the group;
'fuck' is several notches up the scale;
'twat' tends to have more venom behind it;
'wanker' has caught up in terms of popularity;
and 'cunt', which is really only used by those intentionally seeking to cause offence.

Some are still so offended by the C-word, that if used off-handedly and careful note is taken of people's reactions, it can be a good litmus test for what kind of social waters you find yourself swimming in.

Barely a flinch and you're among liberals; if you find your drink in your face, you'll know you should have gone with something else.

'SWINGING SIXTIES'

The widespread availability of an oral contraceptive from 1961, the Beatles' onslaught on the hit parade (beginning in 1962), and the rise of pirate radio (starting with Radio Caroline in 1964) all contributed to journalists deciding to label an entire decade.

Soon the whole world had been sold the idea that Britain was The Place To Be. Indeed, over the course of the decade abortion was legalised, the death penalty was abolished, and England won the World Cup.

Despite this idyllic image, during much of the 1960s it still rained a lot, free love generally seemed to happen to someone else, and everything was shut on Sundays. And Wednesday afternoons.

As the now distinctly long-in-the-tooth adage states, if you meet anyone in the UK that can remember the 1960s, chances are he or she wasn't there.

~ ❁ T ❁ ~

TABLE MANNERS

Once, the easiest way to make sure you were never invited to dinner again, would have been to ignore the following rules of dining etiquette:

- Once cutlery is picked up from the table, it must never touch the table again, but should always rest on the plate.
- Dishes should be passed left to right.
- Salt and pepper are always passed together, even if someone only asks you for one.

In recent years, British table etiquette has become a bit of a lost art, though out of politeness, people tend to wait until everyone has been served their food before they commence shovelling.

Indeed, things that used to be considered a hanging offence – placing your elbows on the table, chewing with your mouth open, eating food from the blade of your knife, or spending the entire meal Twittering – would now barely raise an eyebrow from your fellow diners.

Naked dining took off in New York in 2008, and we do like to imitate those Yanks... Just make sure the soup is gazpacho.

TEA

Less a drink than a national institution, the leaves of the *Camellia sinensis* were first brought to Britain by the East India Company in the seventeenth century, and are now most commonly used in the packaged form of the teabag.

More traditionally, a teapot would be used, with a teabag added for each person present, plus an extra teabag 'for the pot', with the additional warming of the pot with hot water first. Purists will insist on the use of (now less common) loose tea leaves in place of the teabags, which then require the use of a tea strainer.

From this point on, the purists split into many rival factions, with various ideas for the precise formula to make a perfect cup of tea. Adding milk while the teabag is in the cup (before or after hot water) is often considered a social faux pas, and, indeed, doing so can change the flavour of the drink for the worse. If making tea with a teapot, adding the milk to the cup first is equally considered a faux pas by some, yet essential by others.

Despite its role in the collective British psyche as a therapeutic source of stress-relief, calm, and peace, when drinking tea be prepared for many cups. Not to mention at least thirty minutes' chat – in tandem with its restorative powers tea has an implicit association with putting the world to rights.

TERRITORIES

At the height of its influence, Great Britain was in possession of an Empire on which the 'sun never set'. As of 2010, that is technically still true – its territories may now number fourteen, but they are spread wide across the world.

For the record, they are:

Anguilla
Bermuda
the British Antarctic Territory
the British Indian Ocean Territory

the British Virgin Islands
the Cayman Islands
the Falkland Islands
Gibraltar
Montserrat
St Helena and Dependencies (Ascension Island and Tristan da Cunha)
the Turks and Caicos Islands
the Pitcairn Islands
South Georgia and South Sandwich Islands
Sovereign Base Areas on Cyprus

The Channel Islands (Guernsey and Jersey) and the Isle of Man have their own constitutional relationship with the UK, but are still under sovereignty of the British Crown.

You probably wouldn't want to wake up in most of them, though Bermuda does have spectacular beaches, and many of the others happen to offer excellent offshore banking services.

THATCHER (BARONESS MARGARET)

The 'Iron Lady'. Prime minister of Britain for the Conservative Party from 1979 to 1990, she took the Conservative Party more to the political right than it had ever been before, opposed the trade unions, and promoted the British ethic of working for yourself rather than the greater good.

Not content with that, she initiated the privatisation of a number of national institutions, made funding cuts the Arts world is still reeling from, and was forced to resign after opposing full European monetary and economic union.

Her name (particularly among liberals) is synonymous with the 'bad old times', despite the fact many people hold that she was instrumental in the fall of the Eastern Bloc.

That all said, she is still the only woman Britain has seen as prime minister *and* leader of the Conservative Party, and so many hold her in high regard for her strong leadership such a predominantly male political scene.

THERAPY

In 2010, the *Observer* reported that, since the early 1990s, the UK has seen a 200 per cent increase in the number of antidepressants prescribed, but a 2.1 per cent increase in the number of people diagnosed with a 'common mental disorder'.

It used to be said that the UK was ten years behind the US, if not in terms of actual technologies, then in terms of attitudes, and there are still some that never entirely made it across the pond. The belief that others will feel comfortable with your decision to share details of a trip to the psychiatrist/therapist/analyst is one of them.

The recent experiences of the armed forces, and the recognition of Post Traumatic Stress Disorder as a legitimate condition, have done much to alleviate any 'unmanly' connotations associated with the decision to seek or accept therapy. Nonetheless, the idea generally remains in the UK that therapy is for the mad.

Considering how relatively poor the British are at expressing their emotions, adopting the US (or indeed European) attitude that talking about your problems with someone emotionally disconnected from you is a Good Thing, and so seeking counsel from a therapist rather than a bottle, might do us all a lot of good.

THOU & YOU

Much like the French, there used to be two ways of saying 'you' in English, *thou* and *you*. In French, using *vous* to someone shows respect, and formality, while using *tu* is a sign of informality.

It was the same with English: the formal *thou*, and informal *you* – indeed, using *you* when you should be using *thou* was hugely disrespectful. Over time, we gradually lost the formal *thou*, with its derivatives *thee* and *thine*, and people now only tend to use them when they want to sound poetic.

TIPPING

It isn't a normal practice in Britain to tip in pubs or cafés; bars, on the other hand, will often return your change on a metal dish, an unsubtle hint to leave some as a tip.

Even the smallest journey in a taxi will require rounding the amount up to the nearest pound, if you don't want your driver to grumble.

In restaurants, a 'discretionary' 12.5 per cent is often added to bills, but a Brit will generally leave the gratuity on. The extra effort to have it removed, and the embarrassment carried with such a request, usually means that even if the service has been terrible, nothing will be said by those at the table.

But they will spend the rest of the evening complaining bitterly about it.

TOILET MONKEYS

A derogatory name for the people paid to work in the bathrooms of nightclubs. Apparently under the assumption that patrons are unable to cope by themselves, club management pay these workers to stand in a toilet all night dealing with the drunk and drugged, squirting soap into patrons' hands, and handing them paper towels to dry their hands with.

They also guard a vast array of aftershaves, perfumes, deodorants, chewing gum, and sweets that patrons may help themselves to, if they pay a tip for the aforementioned help.

A metal plate suggestively filled with pound coins often sits nearby, mercilessly playing on the British sense of protocol, etiquette, and politeness:

> To receive help washing your hands and *not* pay a tip: the height of rudeness.
>
> To try to wash your own hands without help: impossible.
>
> To help yourself to aftershave or a lollipop without leaving a tip: tantamount to stealing a child.

As such, the only course of action is to leave as quickly as possible, avoiding eye-contact and the hand-basin at all costs.

TOLERANCE

Despite much grandstanding from politicians on the subject of immigration on one side, and a rise in the popularity of right-wing movements on the other, the UK strives to maintain a reputation for tolerance throughout the world. As a result, Britain is seen as a haven for those are who looking to flee intolerance, repression, and persecution.

It remains a land with a vigorously free press, a legal system accessible to most if not all, and a populace who will tend to be polite about the most controversial of opinions, at least for as long as the person espousing them is present.

TOLLS

The price you pay in the UK for a relative lack of toll roads is masses of traffic at every turn, and indeed, every straight. So the small stretches of motorway and major bridges and crossings where tolls do apply are a relative pleasure to drive along.

A norm in Europe, toll roads in the UK are the exception: the Dartford Crossing on the M25 in Kent, the Severn Crossing on the M4 from Bristol into Wales, the Forth Road Bridge on the A90 in Scotland, the Mersey and Tyne Tunnels.

The most recent toll road, a splinter-stretch of the M6, hasn't really put a dent in the commuter jams that build up around Birmingham's spaghetti junction. This is probably down to the fact that many Brit drivers would far rather spend hours sitting in traffic on a perfectly decent, much longer route, for free, than waste good money on a toll road.

TWINNED TOWN

Introduced in the wake of World War I in an attempt to broaden understanding of other nations' cultures and societies, the twinning of towns is a practice that continues today throughout Europe.

While critics of the scheme claim it has no discernible effect on anything or anyone, anywhere, it does ensure that even the most

travel-shy of Brits can name at least one other place in Europe that isn't within twenty minutes' drive of their own front door.

Even if they can't pronounce it correctly.

'TYPICAL'/TUTTING

A particularly British summation of a turn of events, the word 'typical' affirms the key principles of 'c'est la vie' more concisely (though perhaps less lyrically). But in order to completely dismiss something out-of-hand, you can tut.

For the vast majority of Brits, tutting is (not the style of dancing that mimics the appearance of human figures on Egyptian hieroglyphics, but) the noise you make when your bus is late, your gestures at a bar are ignored, or your toast is burnt.

Made by sucking the tip of the tongue back away from the teeth through pursed lips, the sound is best served with a side order of rolled eyes and a dismissive sneer, while mentally repeating the word 'typical'.

ULSTER

The name comes from the Ulaid tribe, the chief inhabitants of the north-eastern part of Ireland. The plantation (or organised colonisation) by British Protestants of the nine Catholic counties of Ulster in the early part of the seventeenth century is at the heart of the civil wars and troubles that have plagued the region. Regardless of what side of the argument you happen to be on, as with much of Britain's colonial expansion, this was not what you might call our finest hour.

UNCLES AND AUNTS

While the technical definition of being either of these people is the same in Britain as everywhere else in the world, a blood tie is often not essential for the honorific to be awarded.

Even if their parents have no actual brothers or sisters, children may have upwards of a dozen 'uncles' and 'aunts' – ranging from godparents and close friends of the family, to the local shopkeeper, next door neighbours, and the guy who stands at the end of the road counting car number plates.

UNIONS

Once famous for their world-class levels of industrial action, British unions enjoy smaller memberships and subsequently less power than in their 1960s and 1970s heyday.

Once, they could effectively hold the nation (and administrations) to ransom. They still remain a force to be reckoned with, and their increasing distance from the Labour Party is likely to add to their level of militancy.

The unions are particularly famous for their picket lines – the human physical barriers formed by union members in order to discourage other workers from starting their shifts.

The UK's largest union is Unite, and its 2,000,000 members do everything from processing nuclear waste to packaging soft drinks. Hopefully not at the same time.

UNITED KINGDOM

There are a number of names ascribed to the lands that comprise the countries of England, Ireland, Scotland, and Wales, together with their outlying isles. So the answer to 'What is this place called?' will depend on your reason for asking the question.

Geographically, the lands are known as the *British Isles*.

Politically they are known as the *United Kingdom of Great Britain and Northern Ireland*: the southern part of Ireland is a republic, and so while the land mass is part of the British Isles, the Republic is not part of the United Kingdom. Northern Ireland is, however, politically a part of the UK, a transition which gave rise to the 'troubles' in the twentieth century.

The land also has been known as *Albion* (from the latin *albus* = white, after the white cliffs of Dover), and *Britannia*. The *Great* of *Great Britain* goes back to the time when Brittany in northern France was under British rule, and was known as *Britannia minor* (as opposed to *Britannia major*).

Very few British people seem to know the reasons for, and the difference in meaning between, these various terms, so for the record, here they are:

The British Isles comprise four separate countries:

> England
> Ireland
> Scotland
> Wales

These four countries have joined together in different ways over the last few hundred years:

1707 – the political union of Scotland and England = *Kingdom of Great Britain*

1801 – the political union of Great Britain and Ireland = *United Kingdom of Great Britain and Ireland*

1922 – twenty-six of Ireland's thirty-two counties separate from the UK, forming the Irish Free State (Republic of Ireland) = *United Kingdom of Great Britain and Northern Ireland*

UP HELLY AA

One of Britain's biggest fire festivals and torch processions, Up Helly Aa has been held in Shetland since 1881. At the end of January, the people of Shetland remember the Viking invasions of a thousand years before.

Some dress up as their conquerors in full costume (the Jarl Squad, with the Guizer Jarl their leader) and a model longship is built. They then drag the ship through the town to the sea, before hurling their torches onto the vessel and creating an almighty bonfire.

Brilliant stuff.

URINALS

If, when entering a male toilet, you choose a urinal next to one already being used, you're committing a British social faux pas.

Even if you observe the unspoken personal space rule, and choose the urinal as far away from the other person as possible, there will be an awkwardness similar to sharing a lift with a stranger.

You must not start a conversation, unless it is a passing comment about (a) sport, (b) the weather, or (c) how much you've had to drink, and how drunk you feel.

~ ❊ **V** ❊ ~

VG

Very Good. A somewhat twee rating used by those harking back to schooldays, and the written praise received with a tick from their teacher in an exercise book. The acronym passed into widespread use after Helen Fielding's *Bridget Jones* books (and subsequent films) became a nationwide phenomenon, and, for some, sadly, never passed out again.

VICAR

A leader of the church, but the exact meaning changes depending on the circumstance. In the Church of England, it means 'someone who is acting as the priest, in place of the rector (who is the head of the parish)'.

In theatrical comedies written in the 1960s, the vicar is the person whose trousers always fall down when a semi-naked woman walks into the room.

WATERLOO

Probably more famous in popular culture as a 1970s song, or the district of London that houses one of the capital's major train stations. The Battle of Waterloo (present-day Belgium) in 1815 saw the Duke of Wellington, soon to become prime minister of Britain, beat Napoleon Bonaparte and end his rule in France as Emperor.

Wellington famously described the battle as 'a damned nice thing – the nearest-run thing you ever saw in your life', a terrifically British and bluff understatement if ever there was one.

WAVING

Brits consider it a prime requisite of all British hosting to see their guests off properly, and it can be a somewhat intimidating affair if you're not used to it. Expect your hosts to follow you out of their own front door and onto the street to your car, regardless of the weather conditions.

At the point when you get into your car (by which time the embraces and handshakes should at least be less frequent) the waving can begin. Like the light in a fridge, you'll never actually see the waving stop – your hosts will not cease waving until you've disappeared from their view.

With this in mind it's probably best to bring the pantomime to an end as promptly as possible: don't worry about normally essential pre-departure tasks like tuning the radio, putting on your seat belt, or releasing the handbrake.

Just get the hell out of there.

WEATHER >> RAIN

'WEE'

A Scottish adjective suggesting something 'small', that has become popular throughout the UK, and which (like 'quite' and 'quick') can often mean anything but 'small'. A 'wee walk round the loch' might prove a challenge for the hardiest of explorers, and a 'wee drink' may well leave you with a headache in the morning.

WELSH RAREBIT

Essentially, Welsh Rarebit (or Rabbit) is the Welsh version of cheese-on-toast, or the French *croque monsieur*. Cheese (usually Cheddar) is melted over toasted bread, with optional additions of pepper, paprika, or other spices.

WESSEX

Like Middlesex, the old county of Wessex only really exists in name. Middlesex was one of many historic counties conceptually banished from the map when it was incorporated into London in 1965. Wessex, meanwhile, hasn't had official status since William the Conqueror had the idea that a boat trip followed by a prolonged punch-up might be a nice way to round off the summer of 1066: he then promptly divided Wessex up between his followers.

Essentially around where Dorset is now, the name still looms large both in the British subconscious and worldwide, largely due to the literature of Thomas Hardy, a self-proclaimed son of Wessex and exceptional writer (despite his seeming phobia about writing anything with a nice happy ending).

WHISPERING

Like audibly breaking wind, jumping red lights, peeing in a swimming pool, or lying to *Big Issue* sellers that you already have that edition, whispering is a low-level social crime best avoided in the UK.

A hangover of Victorian etiquette, it is still considered by some as bad manners to whisper in public. However, in a similar vein to the four offences mentioned above, whispering is something everyone has done at some time or another, and the main thing is to not get caught doing it.

'WHITE VAN MAN'

The WVM is a marketing construct which has passed into popular parlance. Shorthand for a certain kind of individual who would once have been labelled 'working class', the WVM's manually skilled employment/own firm ensures he earns more than a traditional white collar office employee.

Tending (very slightly) to the right of centre politically, there is a generally held view that he reads the *Sun* newspaper, enjoys all-inclusive package holidays, and drives aggressively and/or inconsiderately. While naturally considering himself the best driver on the road.

WIGS (LEGAL)

The bigger the wig, the higher the legal standing. Judges' wigs will stretch down past their shoulders. By comparison, the wigs of barristers will barely reach their ears. This presumably allows the judge to hide the earphones, muffling the pleas and arguments of the concerned parties and their counsels, and enjoy a nice nap until adjournment time.

WILDLIFE

Britain doesn't really have any *wild*life, in its truest sense. There are relatively wild horses in and around the New Forest, while the UK's

only venomous snake – the adder – is the size of a short shoelace, and packs the poisonous capabilities of a bumble bee (though people have died from both adder bites and bee stings).

Perhaps this vacuum at the top of the ferocious beasts table is what has led to the cows making their claim for the title. Cattle-related fatalities are increasingly common – in the last ten years around 500 people have been injured or killed in 'bovine incidents'.

WILLIAM WALLACE

The rebel warrior with a fondness for body paint and, since the 1990s Oscar-winning movie, an Australian lilt to his accent. Details of the life of William Wallace are difficult to pick out from the murk created by an epic poem written nearly 200 years after his death by the poet Blind Harry. Wallace's height, strength, and fighting ability were all exaggerated and became the stuff of legend.

What's certain is that Wallace's assault on English tyranny at the tail end of the thirteenth century, though ultimately doomed, no doubt helped destabilise an already precarious situation for the English King Edward I. Once the Guardian of Scotland, Wallace's capture and (gruesome) execution did little more than confirm his mythic status in Scottish hearts forever.

WIMBLEDON (ALL ENGLAND LAWN TENNIS ASSOCIATION)

Britain may not have produced a world number one player since Abba were in the recording studio, but its love affair with the back-and-forth sport of tennis remains undiminished.

The focal point for tennis lovers since 1877, queues for tickets at the summer Wimbledon competition now begin the night before a match, and vast demand ensures that visitors can expect to pay a premium price just to enter the complex.

In recent years, tennis fans unable to make it onto an actual court can join the crowds in front of a giant video screen that has been erected

at the bottom of a nearby hill. The land feature's name changes in tandem with whichever luckless individual is charged with carrying the UK's hopes for seeing a Brit crowned champion: it was once called Henman Hill, and is currently known as Murray Mound.

WINDSOR

A town and a name. The town is the home of Eton College, Royal Ascot, and Windsor Castle – one of the Queen's five official royal residences. The name has a different story to tell.

Windsor has been the name of the British Royal Family only since 1917. Before that time, King George V was a member of the House of Saxe-Coburg und Gotha. This was felt to be 'inappropriately Germanic', considering the World War, and George signed a declaration changing the House name to Windsor.

WORLD HERITAGE SITES

While Britain may have trouble keeping up with the rest of the world in a whole host of areas, it does history rather well. This is reflected in both the number and quality of World Heritage Sites to be found on these isles.

A visit to any is time well spent, but special mention should go to The Giant's Causeway (in County Antrim), Stonehenge (in Wiltshire), Caernarfon Castle (in North Wales), and the group of neolithic monuments that comprise the Heart of Neolithic Orkney (off the coast of Scotland). As of 2010, there were twenty-eight World Heritage Sites in total, spreading the length and breadth of Britain, with many more waiting to be added to the list.

'WOTCHA'

'What cheer be with you?' became far too much of a mouthful for the average Brit several hundred years ago. The shortened version echoes more modern informal greetings such as 'What are you up to?' or 'What you doing?' and remains a part of the popular British greeting parlance, albeit one with a distinctly nostalgic, or even childish flavour.

X RATED (CENSORSHIP)

We're still only a relatively short period away from a time in Britain when kissing in public was thought to be disgusting, and holding hands was seriously frowned upon.

The most daring of the *Carry On...* films in the 1950s and 1960s were described as 'saucy' for implying sexual shenanigans, as if the public considered humans to be absolutely pure of mind and innocent of virtue.

Culturally speaking, violent or sexual content still provokes furious debate and complaint, with some instances incurring the wrath of the Censors.

As recently as the mid-twentieth century, stage-plays had to be submitted to the Lord Chamberlain's office for approval, while the British Board of Film Classification (formerly of Film Censorship) continues to classify films that are intended to be theatrically shown in this country (although local councils can make their own decisions, they tend to follow the BBFC).

The campaigner Mary Whitehouse fought against what she considered to be a lack of morals and decency on television in the latter half of the twentieth century, while the theatre critic Kenneth Tynan helped considerably in the fight for the removal of censorship from British theatres in the 1960s.

As for print, Britain hasn't banned a book since the 1980s (former MI5 officer Peter Wright's secret-revealing autobiography *Spycatcher*) and is moving towards a generally more liberal-minded society.

꙳ ❖ **Y** ❖ ꙳

YORKSHIRE

A beautiful part of the country famous for a dying mining industry, a fashion sense that hasn't changed since Monty Python made jokes about it in the 1960s, and a pudding that's served with beef gravy.

The people of the area unfairly have a reputation for being bloody-minded (stubborn), producing world-class sportsmen, and very

good beer. One of its most famous exports, the Yorkshire pudding, is a staple part of a Sunday Roast, with a level of deliciousness unparalleled in savoury food. Just try one.

'YUPPIE'

A term that hasn't been used in the UK since the late eighties, and one that doesn't look like it'll be making a comeback any time soon. An extension of the acronym for Young Urban (or Upwardly Mobile) Professional, the term was used for ambitious, mobile-phone wielding, City-dwelling, fast-car driving bankers who wanted to be Michael Douglas in the 1987 film *Wall Street*.

✽ Z ✽

ZEBRA CROSSINGS

A UK invention that's been exported around the world, Zebra crossings allow pedestrians to put courtesy and/or eyesight to the test. By walking out onto the striped area of road that defines them, they put enormous faith into the notion that drivers will stop their vehicles.

This would be seen as utterly ridiculous almost anywhere else in the world, but in Britain, it works. The stripes give the crossing its name, while in place of traffic lights sit Belisha beacons (after the government minister who introduced them).

Along with the Zebra, the most common of the UK's five different types of crossing is the Pelican. Unlike the Zebra it compels drivers to stop, by means of a button-operated traffic light. This gives pedestrians the right of way indisputably, and may explain why they have a tendency to smugly dawdle when crossing. But you can bet the engines will start to rev when the lights begin to change.

Britain also boasts Puffin (as the Pelican, but with sensors that detect pedestrians and a near-side traffic light), Toucan (for bicycles as well as pedestrians), and Pegasus crossings (for horses).

We told you we're a funny bunch.